Is it Just Me or is Modern Football S**t?

IS IT JUST ME OR IS MODERN FOOTBALL S**T?

An Encyclopaedia of Everything That is Wrong in the Modern Game

Jim Keoghan

First published by Pitch Publishing, 2021

Pitch Publishing
A2 Yeoman Gate
Yeoman Way
Worthing
Sussex
BN13 3QZ
www.pitchpublishing.co.uk
info@pitchpublishing.co.uk

A CIP catalogue record is available for this book
from the British Library.

ISBN 978-1 78531773 6

Typesetting and origination by Pitch Publishing

Printed and bound in India by Replika Press Pvt. Ltd.

Chapters

To Nicky, Jamie and Emma.

Because you are everything to me

Acknowledgements

I WOULD like to say a big thanks to everyone who helped with this book, most notably Bev, Rob and Mike, with whom I've spent the past few years navigating the ups and downs of the modern game.

Also, a big thanks to my brother-in-law, Aiden, who produced a cover so much better than anything I could have imagined. Particularly impressive considering how lightweight and poorly described was the brief I gave him.

At Pitch Publishing I'm grateful to Paul and Jane for giving me this opportunity and would like to thank everyone else there who has been involved in the creation of the book.

On a personal level, my children, Emma and Jamie, have provided a welcome and much needed distraction from the daily grind of writing. And even though they've monopolised my computer during the many lockdowns of the past year, meaning that I've had to write this book in snatched moments, it has been a joy to have them around more.

But I save my biggest thanks, as always, for Nicky, without whom there would be no book. I don't know where I would be without your love and unconditional support. Still not nearly enough cups of tea (if any). But then, you can't have it all.

Introduction

MODERN FOOTBALL™ eh? It's a bit s**t isn't it?

Selfies, fan-cams, massive dancing mascots, Jesse Lingard, signature celebrations, corporate partnerships, escalating ticket prices, Jesse Lingard, half-scarves, Fan TV, celebrity refs, Jesse Lingard ...

It's not like the good old days. You remember them, right? When football was still the 'People's Game'. That halcyon era when it only cost two groats to get in and the players earned less than a welder.

But those days are gone now. Blown out of existence by the shiny world of modern football.

Of course, you don't want to get too 'Yer Da' about this. Football has always evolved. That evolution might have occurred at a more glacial pace prior to the arrival of the Premier League in 1992, but it took place, nonetheless. Rule changes, the arrival of TV, the abolition of the maximum wage – the game has possessed its own momentum since inception, one that restlessly sought change and improvement.

And even after 1992, as what we now refer to as modern football began to assert itself, not every change ushered in has been an unwelcome one.

I might look back on my first faltering footsteps as a fan in the early 1980s through rose-tinted specs, but I'm aware enough to recognise that what I experienced was no footballing utopia. The crush of the terraces, the language used that should never be used, the absence of consideration for anyone smaller than 6ft and not built like a brick s**thouse.

And the play! It's a good idea to never look back at videos of the once great teams from your club's past. In your memories you imagine them like Pep-era Barcelona, a whirling symphony of pass and move. But just a few minutes watching the long balls launched and the hit-and-hope crosses quickly disabuses you of this notion.

For all its ills, the game today, at almost every level of the sport, is technically and tactically better than it was in the pre-1992 age. The players are fitter, better trained, more astute and, at the higher levels of football, drawn from the brightest and best of the world. In the days before the Premier League rolled into town, a club was considered to have a broad, international reach if they had more than one Scandinavian in their team.

And it still remains the game that we love, a game that continues to move us in ways that so few things can. For many of us, football, even in its modern guise, is something that we find it hard to live without, a reality that was made clear when the sport was temporarily suspended during the first coronavirus lockdown in 2020. Many fans were left bereft by the pause, untethered by the sudden absence of the season's cut and thrust. We might moan about the way football has changed, but few of us would be without it.

Despite this and the obvious improvements that have taken place, there's undoubtably a sense that modern football comes at a cost. For a generation of fans, most commonly those who have lived through the slow death of the pre-1992 world, there's a feeling that it's a cost that's often quite hard to bear.

Massive financial inequality, selfie-obsessed supporters, Michael Owen as a pundit – the crimes of the modern game are seemingly limitless. But a few definitely grate more than most. Which is where this book comes in, your guide to some of the worst things about the game today. It's not an exhaustive list, and you might not agree with every inclusion, but it should provide enough examples to probably answer the question: Is it just me, or is modern football s**t?

A4 Protests

Picture yourself as the owner of a Premier League football club. You can choose what kind; sleazy Russian oligarch, reputation-washing Middle Eastern sheik or an asset-sweating, dead-eyed American automaton.

Now also imagine that the club is going through a rocky patch and there are rumblings that the crowd is turning against you. In your darkest moments, you picture in your mind something akin to the storming of the Winter Palace at the next home game, vast swathes of the great unwashed crashing against the directors' box.

Imagine your relief then when you take your seat to find that these 'rumblings' have merely amounted to a few fans holding up dog-eared pieces of A4 paper, upon which messages of protest have been hastily scribbled. Sipping on your expensive cognac, your feet resting upon the back of a crouching steward, you bathe in relief, letting your mind shift to more pleasurable considerations, such as which artisan cheese you'll opt for at half-time.

The construction of these signs represents a rare example in the game of deliberate, premeditated s**tness. Not for them the organised mass protest or the sophisticated online campaign. Not even the slickly produced banner. This is the 'f**k it' approach – minimal input for minimal impact.

And frequently you wonder whether they've even read the sign back. Multiple fonts and capital letters in the wrong place, they sometimes look more like the kind of letter a serial killer might send to the police to taunt them about their lack of progress in the ongoing manhunt.

Can it work? Will any owner ever stare down into the crowd, see this 'protest' and the look of solemnity the protestor usually wears when holding the sign aloft and think, 'You know what? I was going to treat this club as my personal plaything and possibly ruin it in the process. But after reading that, I think it's about time I changed my ways.'?

In an infinite universe filled with infinite possibilities, it could happen. But I think it's asking a lot of those signs. Far more likely instead that the sleazy chairmen of football's grim future will get to enjoy their artisan cheese in peace.

Advertising Hoardings

Back in December 2017, one-time wunderkind and current Lille midfielder, Renato Sanches, then playing for Swansea City, made headlines when he mistakenly passed the ball to an advertising hoarding during a game against Chelsea.

The on-loan Bayern Munich man (he gets around) had collected the ball in the centre circle, looked up, and passed off to his left. Only there was no team-mate there to receive. To the disgust of his fellow players and the crowd, the ball rolled out of play, hitting a hoarding displaying the Carabao logo.

Sanches later said that he had confused the logo for one of his team-mates, which was a worrying claim considering it featured the white skull of a carabao. Unless he was under the misapprehension that Peter Crouch had recently signed for the club, it's difficult to understand who Sanches had in mind when he did this.

Although widely mocked for his mistake, it's hard not to feel some sympathy for the young midfielder. Back in the pre-digital age, advertising hoardings were simple things. No flashing lights or moving images, they were constant and sedate, advertising straightforward, local things, such as processed meat and scaffolding.

In the modern game, thanks to the arrival of LED lights, they now represent an ocular assault. Always changing, brightly lit, sometimes containing a moving image, these new hoardings are a constant distraction. Not only is it easy to see why Sanches was momentarily confused, it's surprising it doesn't happen more often.

The lead offender in this distracting trend is unquestionably Stanley the Dachshund. You probably know 'Stanley' by his other, more commonly used names, which include: 'Is that a dog on the pitch?' 'There's that dog again', and 'Why is that f**king dog still there?' He was created to advertise Vitality insurance, who somehow thought that pissing off as many football fans as possible would be a good way to rustle up some business.

Despite the advancement in technology, it's debatable whether Stanley and his ilk are even necessary anyway. For years, the printed hoardings of the past worked their subliminal magic. Ever had a craving for a Mars bar as you're viewing a game on TV? An inexplicable desire for scaffolding while at the match? A sudden, visceral memory of Peter Crouch while watching the League Cup?

But they can't leave things alone, always trying to find new ways to make us buy more stuff. And who is the ultimate victim in all of this? Who suffers the most? Well, it's poor little Renato, a man who will forever be known as the first footballer in history to try to play a through pass to a carabao, a mantle that will haunt him wherever he goes for years to come.

Football Agents

Agent is a strange word. When you add it to others, it has the unique knack of making the combination instantly more unpleasant. Take the word 'estate', innocuous enough. Now add the word 'agent' and feel your skin begin to crawl.

The same is true of 'orange', entirely harmless on its own. Now stick 'agent' in front of it and suddenly you have the health-wrecking herbicide used by the US Army during the Vietnam War, one that spread devastation and misery wherever it was sprayed.

Another kind of agent that spreads devastation and misery wherever they're sprayed are football agents.

They started out, about a generation ago, as innocent representation for players, helping protect the best interests of individuals whose skill set was better equipped for chasing a ball around a pitch than sitting around a negotiating table, sifting through the finer points of contractual law.

The first agent to really break through into the popular consciousness was Eric Hall, who in his 90s pomp represented the likes of Dennis Wise, Neil Ruddock and Tim Sherwood. He was a larger-than-life personality who seemed to apply a level of discernment to his client base, very much rooted in the 'arsehole' category.

But for all his surface slipperiness, with his limited domestic reach, he seems a bit quaint from today's vantage point. Nowadays, there's so much more to the agent game, particularly as a small group of so-called 'super agents' effectively run the whole transfer market, pulling it in the direction they choose. These people can build entire teams; they can also pull them apart. They can make clubs pay way more than they would want to. And you're taking a huge gamble if you decide to cross them.

Agents like Mino Raiola, representative of Paul Pogba, Zlatan Ibrahimović and Erling Haaland. Once described by Alex Ferguson as a 's**tbag', Raiola has come a long way since his early days of delivering pizza for his parents' restaurant in the Netherlands. Although even back then the seeds of his future career were apparent, with Raiola eating a 10 per cent cut from every pizza delivered and frequently briefing the local press about the pizza's desire to be delivered to a different house.

Raiola and co. excel at exploiting the 24-hour news machine, feeding it rumours and half-hearted denials. They keep the transfer gossip columns churning all year round, seeding hints and false hope, toying with our emotions, all with the aim of improving their leveraging position.

They might not be as clean and creepy as estate agents or quite as capable of deforestation as Agent Orange, but the power and influence of these agents is still one of modern football's more depressing developments. Somehow, the people who make the deals have become almost as important as the players they represent.

Armchair Scouts

Beyond the big names and those you saw on a regular basis, there used to be a sense of ignorance about a lot of footballers. In the analogue days of the past, so little was known about many players that often, when a signing was mooted, they were a bit of an unknown quantity.

That was particularly the case with those from beyond our shores. The international scene was like a footballing black hole, an information void from which foreign players would emerge, with their exquisitely coiffured mullets, their outlandish fashion sense and their bewilderment at the English footballer's contention that midweek benders represented a legitimate addition to any sensible training schedule.

And underlining it all, a lingering sense of deference towards clubs, a belief that they might know more about recruitment than us fans. Scouting was shrouded in mystery, a world of gut feelings and crafty bines.

But not anymore. Nowadays, everybody is a f**k-ing expert.

When Real Madrid signed proto-starlet, Martin Ødegaard from the backwoods of Norwegian football in 2015, within hours of the deal being announced a tsunami of articles about his potential poured forth from the keyboards of football's modern army of armchair scouts.

They trawl the stats and watch the clips, knocking out opinion pieces with a veneer of quasi-scientific inquiry.

But can you really just set yourself up as an expert without the training or years of experience? Can I just decide tomorrow to become a surgeon because I've sat through a season of *Holby City*? Or become a police detective after watching old episodes of *Columbo*? Sure, I can wear a dirty mac and smoke a cigar, but can I really ingratiate myself into Martin Landau's confidence and then use his own sense of overconfidence against him to reveal to the world that he killed his wife?

I know we're meant to live in an age where information has been democratised and the public enjoy a Govean dislike of 'experts', but might it still be the case that the people who scout for a living, those hardy souls who have spent their lifetimes watching game after game, player after player, all in the hope of unearthing a gem, might know more than the blogger who spent five minutes watching a YouTube highlights reel?

And maybe in a game as predictable as modern football often is, it also just makes a nice change to be surprised for once. To have the opportunity, without prejudice, to witness a Per Krøldrup defensive masterclass or to savour the goalscoring impotence of Vincent Janssen, free from preconceptions. To luxuriate in the ineptitude of Jan Kromkamp, without prior knowledge.

Sometimes, blissful ignorance is best.

Autobiographies

Part of the problem with many modern football autobiographies is the fact that most of the players in question haven't had that much of a life to begin with. Wayne Rooney's first autobiography, *My Story So Far*, came out when he was 20. What are we really going to learn from that? His love of chicken dippers? How many times he's been to Alton Towers? Autobiographies work best when it's an elder statesperson looking back over a long life well lived, not someone fresh out of school reminiscing about their favourite ninja turtle.

And then there's the often-tedious life of a footballer to consider. These aren't musicians regaling us with stories of drug-fuelled benders or actors indulging in a bit of 'kiss-and-tell'. They're professional athletes who have spent most of their adult lives keeping in good physical shape and doing the same thing, week in, week out, which is as boring as it sounds.

The masterwork in the tedious autobiography genre is unquestionably Sami Hyypiä's *From Voikkaa to the Premiership*. No entertaining stories and nothing about what shaped or motivated him. Instead, a description, in painstakingly tedious detail, of his progression from the Finnish town of Voikkaa to the Premier League. It's best to think of it less as an autobiography and more of a sleep aid, like a stronger version of Temazepam (caution: side effects include thoughts of self-harm and an irrational hatred of Finns).

Footballers also live in something of a bubble, cushioned from the harsh realities of life by the protective embrace of the club. Inevitably, this can occasionally create unsympathetic figures, whose perceived injustices and petty point-scoring leave a bad taste in the mouth of those unfortunate enough to have wasted their money on their magnum opus.

The go-to benchmark for the unsympathetic memoir will always be Ashley Cole's *My Defence*, a tome that might have been better titled *Detailed Reasons Why You Should Hate Me*. Cole spends great swathes of the book railing against the financial injustices that were inflicted upon him, such as the horror of being a 19-year-old earning just £25,000. The lesson of the book seems to be that Cole's life would have been so much better if only people had given him the vast amounts of money he thought he was worth.

But at least his title, with its play on words, was relatively imaginative. The same can't be said for so many others in this genre.

Most are hopelessly simplistic: *My Life in Football* – Robbie Fowler, *A Life in Football* – Ian Wright, *My Life in Football* – Kevin Keegan. It doesn't bode well for the book if the first words, those that are meant to draw you in, have all the pyrotechnic punch of an indoor firework.

Mind you, even when they do put in a bit of thought, the results can be frustrating, like Garry Monk's *Loud,*

Proud and Positive, which, with its LGBTQ connotations, gives the impression of a book that's going to be a lot more sexually revelatory than it really is.

The old adage is that you shouldn't judge a book by its cover. But if you see a picture of a famous footballer on the front, and that cover also contains the word 'autobiography', then judge away and save your money.

B Teams

Never one to look a gift crisis in the mouth, back in the autumn of 2020, as a succession of Football League clubs faced the prospect of financial oblivion in the wake of the coronavirus pandemic, Manchester City's chief executive, Ferran Soriano, called for a rethink of the football pyramid, suggesting that now was the time, at last, to seriously consider the inclusion of Premier League B Teams in the EFL's various divisions.

It was a reworking of an idea that was first mooted back in 2014, which proposed the creation of a new League Three tier for the Football League, made up of Premier League B teams and National League clubs. At the time, the clubs of the EFL voted to reject the plan, believing that the issue had been put to bed. Evidently, it was just dormant. Proponents of the introduction of B Teams tend to use the same seductive language, arguing that the change must be brought in to benefit young English players who find the transition to senior football a challenge without the benefit of a competitive environment, the kind that would be provided by the lower tiers of the Football League. They claim that the B Team plan will, in the long term, benefit the national team too.

But opponents see another motivation, an effort by the Premier League to extend its reach further into the game, potentially syphoning off more supporters from the lower divisions in the process. They argue that maybe if elite teams didn't stockpile so many young players within their academy systems, allowing smaller clubs to recruit them instead, then this problem wouldn't have arisen in the first place.

Fans of the B Team model tend to look to Germany for inspiration, a country where Bundesliga giants, like Bayern Munich, Borussia Dortmund and Hoffenheim have reserve/youth teams playing in lower divisions. 'Look,' they shout, 'it works over there, and everybody loves German football.'

'But don't look too closely,' they continue, 'because you'll probably also see other stuff that works over there, like affordable ticket prices, supporter ownership and effective administrative oversight.'

The problem with any attempt at restructuring the pyramid is that the Premier League bosses are probably the last people on earth anyone should ask for their opinion. It would be a bit like courting Sauron for his view on the right to privacy or asking Fred West to reform local authority building regulations. Their input might well contain some insight, but maybe their motivations are less than pure.

Although, you can't help thinking that it's a case of when rather than if B Teams will enter the Football League. It's something that the elite of the game clearly want and if the past 30 years has taught us anything about English football, it's that when the elite want something, you would be a fool to bet against it happening.

Balls

According to Nike, official ball supplier to the Premier League, the new Merlin ball is inspired by the urban landscapes of England's cities. Which is why, for the first time, we've seen a top-flight football that's decorated with the ravages of Austerity and lone Alsatians.

The marketing for these balls is, ironically, often a load of just that. Nike went on to say that with the Merlin their aim was to 'design a ball that specifically illustrated the traits of Premier League football', which should have made it the first ball in history to be inflated by its own bloated sense of self-importance.

Modern balls do, admittedly, represent an improvement on the brown, leather ones of the past, the kind that used to absorb water like a sponge and that represented the perfect medium to massively improve your chances of developing early onset dementia. But for traditionalists, those who widely believe that football technology reached perfection with the arrival of the Mitre Delta in the 1980s, there's a sense of tinkering for the sake of it.

Do balls really need 'striking colour combinations and a bold new graphic layout providing heightened visual clarity for players'? Before all of this, weren't balls basically white?

Or maybe they're being tinkered with simply to squeeze ever increasing amounts of cash out of us. Considering that these new balls can cost up to £80 for punters to buy, it makes perfect sense for Nike to rubbish everything that has come before and, with seductively scientific language, tell you that this is the only ball that matters now.

But they shouldn't tinker too much. As anyone who has watched sci-fi films in which people meddle with forces beyond their control knows only too well, there's always the chance that things might go wrong when we meddle for the sake of it. It's happened before in football, the sorry tale of Jabulani standing as a cautionary tale.

It arrived courtesy of Adidas for the 2010 World Cup and caused controversy from the very start. At some point, somebody at Adidas thought it a good idea to endow the ball with sentience. And that meant that it, not the player, designated how it would travel. The Jabulani dipped and swerved independently, moving to its own will, causing international goalkeepers to break out in a cold sweat whenever a shot came in.

Since then, FIFA has cautioned against sentient footballs. The organisation is keen to avoid a repeat of the farce that was the 2010 World Cup. But you can't help fearing that now Pandora's box has been opened, it's only a matter of time before another such monstrosity is unleashed upon an unsuspecting world.

Betting Sponsors

There used to be a pervading sense of simplicity, almost innocence, in the relationship between football clubs and their shirt sponsors. Despite the nakedly commercial nature of the partnership, for a long time you never got the sense that clubs were trying that hard.

Although the game was already on the path to the moral-free vacuum that we see today, back when the Premier League launched in 1992, a hint of this idyllic age was still, just about, apparent. Such as at Sheffield United, who were sponsored by Laver, a Yorkshire timber merchant. Or a few hundred miles further south, Southampton boasting the name of Draper Tools on their chests, a family-run business in Hampshire. Both hardly examples of predatory capitalism.

Fast forward a generation and, at the top, the near-unquenchable thirst for income has blown apart any innocence that might once have existed. Football clubs now search long and hard for the best deal possible, irrespective of any local connection or moral considerations.

And that's how we've ended up with so many clubs in the Premier League and the Championship having the name of a betting firm emblazoned on their shirts. During the 2019/20 season, across the two divisions, over half of all clubs had such a sponsorship arrangement.

For anti-gambling campaigners, the betting boom has played a part in the inexorable rise in the number of problem gamblers in the UK, specifically those in their late teens.

But, as bad as this is, things might get a whole lot worse in the years to come. A few years ago, we got a glimpse of what could happen if the growth and expansion of the betting firms isn't challenged. Of all the dystopian futures that have been conjured up by modern fiction, none compares to the terrifying possibility that Bet365 dreamed up back in 2014. It was a world in which its people were ruled by the giant, disembodied head of Ray Winstone.

Like a version of Oz the Great and Powerful but reimagined as a gangland boss with an overactive thyroid, the head would appear, unbidden, insisting through a thinly veiled sense of menace that it would now be 'cushty' for people to gamble their meagre incomes on how many corners Derby County might concede in the following 45 minutes. For in this nightmarish possible future, the 'in-play' governed all, its citizens locked in an endless cycle of joyless live betting.

Inadvertently, the very people who will benefit most from the trend have warned us of its possible implication. This is what we must fight against. The reign of the Great and Powerful Geezer must be resisted at all costs.

A Bigger, Better World Cup

Whether you're talking about bribes, pointless awards ceremonies or cosying up to murderous regimes, FIFA fully embraces the concept of: 'the more the better'.

And nowhere is this thinking more perfectly illustrated than in its decision to expand the number of those playing in the World Cup from 32 to 48 by the time the 2026 competition rolls into town.

With 16 groups made up of three teams (with the top two advancing to a round of 32), the tournament, which will be hosted by the USA, Canada and Mexico, promises to take the sporadic boredom common to the early stages of recent World Cups and expand that on a scale never seen before.

Of all the many column inches written about why this is such a bad idea, none expressed it better than the *Financial Times*'s Moscow correspondent a few years ago, who simply wrote: 'World Cup 2026: The Phantom Menace'. This is the moment when the franchise starts to devour itself.

Of course, Gianni Infantino's decision to widen participation in FIFA's elite tournament *could* be seen as a genuine reach for greater sporting meritocracy, a desire for more countries to know the joy of being knocked out of the World Cup in the early stages. But then again, perhaps he just wants the support of as many football associations as possible and with predicted profits to rise by just over £600m, lots more cash for FIFA. We'll probably never know for sure.

But what we do know is that the new format will come with plenty of downsides, including:

An Endless Draw: If you thought FIFA had mastered the art of the glacial draw ceremony, think again. Past draws are going to seem like a breeze compared to the ones on the horizon. They're going to be so long that some international players will have started and then finished their careers before they're completed.

Boom Time for Leering Perverts: The more games that take place, the more opportunities there will be for the competition's degenerate cameramen to ogle unsuspecting women in the crowd, a weirdly accepted part of World Cup broadcasting. Either the TV companies think their audience is exclusively comprised of sleazy middle-aged men or they're simply hiring these cameramen straight from prison.

Panini Hell: With hundreds of additional players, Panini's sticker books will become so thick and heavy that once completed they'll remain immovable. Over time, like Stonehenge or the giants of Easter Island, they'll become monuments to a past civilisation. Flicking through their faded pages, future generations will wonder how American Samoa made it to the World Cup finals and try to understand just what a Piotr Zieliński was exactly.

oots

(A) Colours

With their lurid hues and names like Predator, Viper and Hypervenom, you would be forgiven for thinking that Nike and Adidas were harbouring a major snake fetish, as though their ranks were ram-jammed with overexcited herpetologists.

Over the last few decades, the once mundane boot, for a long time only available in black, has been given an extensive makeover. Along with an array of sexy snake-themed names, the full colour palette has been poured into design (sometimes all at once).

Zebra-print, khaki camouflage, spotted-pink dots – boot creators have been given free licence, producing a vast array of eye-assaulting designs. At the more outlandish extremes of the boot world, colours clash in a vomity swirl of contrasting shades that seem to have been thrown together without thought.

And they've become ubiquitous. Where once, coloured boots were the sole preserve of the 'flair player', the kind of cocksure luxury who would barely break a sweat during matches, waiting for that one moment of inspiration that often never came, now they're everywhere. In the modern game even the sturdy, unremarkable stalwarts of the defence, the agricultural, no-nonsense centre-halves race around the pitch wearing what looks like a psychedelic explosion on their feet.

And if the names and colours aren't s**t enough …

(B) Construction

It all started with the Adidas Predator back in 1994, the first boot to move away from traditional construction techniques.

Based on a concept dreamed up by the former Liverpool midfielder, Craig Johnston, the Predator incorporated rippled fins that allowed players to impart more power and curve to the ball. To play exactly like Craig Johnston never did.

The technological developments have rolled on since, such as Nike's innovative use of synthetic fibres in the late

1990s and their recent introduction of 'flyknit' uppers, a sort of half sock that absorbs a season's worth of ankle sweat to produce a smell that could be used as a chemical weapon.

So much change has occurred that modern boots almost bear no relation to their heavy, leather forebears.

Here's the problem though. The vast majority of us who buy and wear these boots are s**t. I don't mean the 'can't kick a ball', 'last pick at PE' kind of s**t. But rather, a common-or-garden variety of s**t. We're massively underwhelming footballers who only manage to hold our own because the general level surrounding us is equally s**t.

And yet, on our feet you'll still see boots imbued with cutting-edge technology. Like using the Hadron Collider to tumble your undies, these boots are massively overqualified for the job. We don't need something this sophisticated when most of our game involves launching the ball to a big number nine or kicking the s**t out of the winger we're tasked with marking. But we buy them just the same, paying ever increasing amounts, swayed by sophisticated marketing that convinces us that their inbuilt technology will make us hit the ball like Ronaldo.

Maybe it's time that boot manufacturers were honest, knocking out boots devoid of technology for the footballing hoi polloi.

And let's forget the snake stuff while we're at it. It's time we gave football boots more appropriate names. How about the Adidas 'Poorly Timed Tackle'? The Nike 'Clear it for F**k's Sake!' And who wouldn't want to buy the Puma 'F**king into These'?

Celebrity Referees

They say that the best referees are the ones you don't see. And in the game's early years that was exactly what officials tried to do, employing an array of camouflage techniques to avoid detection.

Perhaps the greatest practitioner of this was Victorian referee, Sir William Harding-Rolls, a man who was able to officiate the 1875 FA Cup Final entirely unseen.

Smothered in green paint, with a single white line running the length of his body, Sir William managed to blend into the touchline, slithering up and down its length on his belly, pausing only to occasionally blow his whistle. It was only when the victorious captain tripped over the unseen Harding-Rolls on his way to collect the trophy that his presence was finally revealed.

It's all a far cry from the modern game, where several referees have become almost as famous as the superstar footballers that they're there to officiate. The likes of Lee Mason, Mike Dean and Martin Atkinson have become household names, as they parade around proceedings, drunk on power and inflated by a disproportionate sense of self-worth.

Two basic characteristics seem common to the 'celeb refs': a monstrous ego and the belief that their duties are at least as important, if not more so, than the actual football on display.

You see them swaggering around the pitch, looking down at the players, belittling skills that pale in comparison to their own.

A sense of 'performance' has crept into the role too, something likely exacerbated by its professionalisation. It's as though now they're getting paid, they have to look like they're doing something more than simply officiating.

Cue an array of overly expressive hand gestures, as they move around the pitch like a polyester Pierrot: the scissor motion across the chest that says 'nothing to see here'; the exaggerated pointing to different parts of the pitch to illustrate why a yellow card has been given; the dismissive flappy hand gesture that tells a player to 'do one'. And worst of all, their greatest piece of pantomime, that weird crouch and squint position that informs the watching public that they've had a really good look at an incident.

In many ways, the emergence of the celebrity referee was inevitable. Over the past 30 years, elite football in this country has received an injection of adrenaline, exaggerating its many foibles and flaws. Referees have become part of this, the worst aspects of the profession blown up to almost comic proportions.

And let's face it, they've always been unusual figures, the kind of people who want to discipline grown men and who radiate an almost homicidal level of psychopathic self-confidence. In modern football, we now have these traits taken to extremes, the very worst of football officialdom prowling around a stage that they think has been primarily built for them, and them alone.

The Champions League

The closing stages of the 2019/20 Champions League had something for everyone. Would you lend your support to the football club/drinks brand marketing strategy, Red Bull Leipzig? Or would you prefer to get behind sportwashing Parisian moneybags PSG? If that wasn't for you, how about the German trophy-gathering juggernaut, Bayern Munich? And last of all, for those searching for a plucky underdog, why not go for Olympic Lyon, the 18th richest club in world football?

The old European Cup had its faults, but it was never this s**t. Only open to actual champions, there was no broadening of the scope to allow the inclusion of teams who finished well off the pace in their domestic leagues. And there was no attempt to exclude those from less glamorous divisions by making them go through numerous, squad-draining qualifying rounds.

To borrow from George Orwell slightly, the Champions League, perhaps more than any other competition in world football, changed all of this by embracing the thinking that all teams are created equal, but some teams are more equal than others.

This is about the European elite, a competition that has been designed to ensure that its closing stages, year in, year out, feature the richest clubs of the Continental game.

So, no more knockouts in the early stages of the competition proper, when in the past a big name having a couple of off-days could find themselves unceremoniously dumped out. And no more chances for weird clubs from weird leagues to get too far, the grinding nature of the qualifying rounds and the group stage slowly draining their will to live.

The group stage itself was perfectly described by 'The Set Pieces' as a 'trough where the big pigs grudgingly share a bit of swill with the little piglets before forcing their snouts down hard into the swirling brown gloop and holding them there until the bubbles stop'.

The whole point is to minimise the risk of upsets and preserve the status quo, boosted by the extended coefficient that protects the big clubs at the start.

And underwriting the whole thing, the foundations upon which UEFA have built their temple of mammon, Financial Fair Play (FFP).

Although introduced, at face value, to stop football clubs chasing success through a debt-fuelled orgy of spending, a pleasant and deliberate side effect for UEFA is the placing of European football in a state of permanent stasis. Without the ability to do a 'Chelsea', it's become more challenging for outsiders to crash into the elite.

Through FFP and the changes made to the format, UEFA have enabled the cream of European football to throw up the city walls and feast on the competition's largesse, confident that those outside have no chance of ever getting in.

And if all of that isn't bad enough, what about that theme tune? A pretentious knock-off of Handel's *Zadok the Priest*, its climatic moment exclaims: Die Meister (The Master), Die Besten (The Best), Les Grandes Equipes (The Great Teams), The Champions. It might be more palatable if they were up front about the reality of the competition.

Maybe this has a better ring to it: Die Selbst Berechtigt (The Self-Entitled), Die Ekelhaft Reich (The Disgustingly Rich), Les Bâtards Avides (The Greedy Bastards), The 'sort of' Champions.

The Checkatrade Trophy

At the time of writing, it should be called the Leasing. Com Trophy, in respect to its latest sponsor. But the EFL Trophy will probably remain known as the 'Checkatrade' for some time to come. It's a title that honours its sponsor when the competition was disastrously overhauled by the EFL back in 2016.

The 'Checkatrade' has been around, under various titles, since the early 1980s, representing a chance for the clubs that make up the bottom two tiers of the Football League to get to Wembley and win a bit of silverware.

With teams from the top two tiers denied entry, even the smallest of clubs with the most stringent budgets still stood a reasonable chance of making it to the final, making it a well-respected competition, blessed with that all-important 'every-outcome-possible' element.

But in 2016, the EFL announced a rebrand, a revamp to the competition that would see development teams from the higher reaches of the pyramid enter into the mix. It was billed as a way to popularise the competition and give young English players from the elite the chance to feature in competitive games, thus helping the future national team.

But it hasn't quite worked out like that. For a start, the changes have, if anything, caused the popularity of the competition to decline sharply. The arrival of a small number of fans from the big clubs has been more than offset by a desertion of those from the lower leagues who have turned their backs on the 'Checkatrade', put off by what they see as an attempt by the Premier League to use the competition as some kind of Trojan Horse for their desire to allow their youth teams to enter the EFL's lower divisions permanently.

In the first year of the competition, attendances plummeted by around a quarter and occasionally broke records along the way. Colchester United saw their lowest ever home crowd, Grimsby saw their lowest ever cup crowd, and the A420 derby (between Oxford and Swindon) saw its lowest ever gate.

And when it came to helping out the national team by giving young English players that all-important competitive blooding, the reality differed somewhat from the theory. In their opening game against Sheffield United, Leicester

City fielded an array of elder statesmen, drawn from across the globe, including a 27-year-old Spanish right-back, a 36-year-old Polish centre-back and a 29-year-old Tunisian centre-back.

Elsewhere in the early rounds, the 25-year-old Portuguese striker Nélson Oliveira was among Norwich's goalscorers. Reading progressed courtesy of goals scored by the 25-year-old Guinea-Bissau forward Joseph Mendes. And Stoke City's only goal in the competition came from one of the hottest young prospects in the English game, Charlie Adam.

Now that they've been allowed to breach the walls of a competition from which they were previously excluded, who knows where the top flight will head next? The Liverpool U14 District Cup? The West Auckland Sunday League? The Brighton and Hove Walking Football Tournament? In their desire to infect as much of English football as possible, the elite's horizons are boundless.

Corporate Partners

I know that you, like me, have spent many lost hours looking at the beautiful face of former Liverpool defender Martin Škrtel, wondering all the time how you too could have skin so pale and waxen.

Well, it turns out that the secret all along was Nivea for Men. Through its simple application, Nivea's advert showed a captivated world that you too could look like the kind of Eastern European rent-a-goon that would die in the first third of a Jason Statham action film.

The campaign, which also featured other Liverpool heart-throbs of the time, Adam Lallana and Philippe Coutinho, formed part of the club's relationship with Nivea, who had recently become Anfield's official men's grooming partner.

It's amazing to think that there was a time when clubs didn't have grooming partners. But it did exist. Perhaps that's why footballers back in the 1970s and 80s looked more like a late-era Keith Richards than athletes in the prime of life.

But since the arrival of corporate football in the 1990s all that has changed. And not just with grooming products. Amongst the self-styled elite, specifically the 'Big Six', corporate partnerships are now as varied as they are inexplicable. Manchester United have an official global oil lubricant and fuel partner, Manchester City an official cyber protection and hybrid cloud storage partner, and Spurs an official global bovine artificial insemination partner.

Apparently, it's all about synergies and sharing strategic goals going forward. And definitely not about whoring out your club's name to as many things as possible as long as it earns a few quid.

The high-water mark, or low point of this trend, depending upon your perspective, is unquestionably the emergence of the various Red Bull teams that now populate world football. A few years ago, the Austrian drinks giant hit upon a novel way to promote their products. Football clubs in the USA, Austria and Germany were taken over and rebranded to carry the Red Bull name. This was corporate football at its most blatant and a horrifying new development in the medium. To paraphrase Red Bull's slogan:

> Red Bull, Gives You Wings (plus the disquieting sense that the future of football is a corporate boot stamping on its face – forever).

Cultivated Atmosphere

Now is the time to provide atmosphere. That's what the high 'NRG' dance music tells you. You hear it at various grounds, pumped out before the teams emerge. The Balearic beats are designed to build up a sense of euphoria, to mimic the E'd-up bliss of the Iberian dancefloor, albeit on a Thursday night. While being rained on. In Sunderland. Sometimes, if you're especially unfortunate, these beats are accompanied by a 'fan-cam', roving over the masses like the Eye of Sauron, singling out individuals who must be in a state of elation under its stare.

All this forms part of 'cultivated atmosphere', football's response to a problem of its own making. It turns out that while the game was congratulating itself on its ability to charge ever increasing amounts of money for punters to come and watch its 'product', it was gradually pricing out the very people responsible for the game's 'legendary' atmosphere.

If you're looking for enthusiasm, passion and a sense of emotional abandonment, the one section of society you should never turn to are middle-aged, middle-class, white men; coincidently, the demographic that football has spent decades chasing.

The easy solution to this problem would be to make football cheaper, bringing the game back to the 'people'. But that would go against everything that is holy for an industry obsessed with the bottom line. The men and women behind our clubs, specifically those that populate the higher reaches of the game, are inured to such an idea. It's as though their brains come equipped with sophisticated filters to block out words that would challenge their worldview – words such as 'affordability', 'inclusiveness' and 'BAME managerial appointments'.

So, what you get instead are sticking plasters, badly thought-out solutions culled from the dream board of the marketing department, like fan-cams, Balearic beats and hand-clappers. Inevitably, it frequently falls flat, leaving grounds, specifically at the top, sounding more like libraries than hubs of passion and excitement.

But perhaps there's a way around this. Maybe those behind these efforts are simply trying to push the wrong emotional buttons. Because if you want to stir the soul of the affluent middle classes to elicit some kind of emotional response, then, as the pages of the *Daily Mail* so expertly illustrate, maybe anger is a better option.

Rather than a fan-cam why not broadcast images on the big screen of ungrateful asylum seekers moving into a suburban semi? Or, instead of those hand-clappers carrying the club crest, maybe as an alternative they could be emblazoned with photos of Diane Abbott. And what better way to ensure that the teams come out to a bubbling cauldron of noise than to replace those 'Balearic beats' with the Islamic call to prayer?

Edgar avids' Uncontrollable Ego

Edgar Davids' eventful stint as player/manager of Barnet a few years ago threw up its fair share of memorable moments. First, there was his 'combative' approach on the pitch, which at one point saw him receive three red cards in a spell of just five games.

Then there was his fairly hefty ego. Not only did the former Juventus midfielder refuse to attend any away games that required an overnight stay, but he also demanded that his players address him as 'sir'.

But most memorable of all was Davids' decision to claim the No.1 shirt. The reasoning was clear: as 'Number One' at the club, why shouldn't he wear the shirt?

For many, the decision represented the final death of the old 1–11. It used to be so easy: 1 in goal, 2–5 at the back, 8 and 9 up top, the rest in midfield. An idiot could understand it. And I did.

But as part of their desire to eradicate football's past, the Premier League ended all of that in the early 1990s. Suddenly it was all about squad numbers, with players sticking to the same number, no matter where or how often they played. And like most of the things invented by the Premier League, where it went, the rest of the game followed.

So now you had No. 23 playing as a 'No. 4', No. 18 playing as a 'No. 9', and a rampant egotist with an unenviable disciplinary record playing in No. 1.

Although Davids is often held up as the worst offender, he's far from the only player whose squad number has struck a dissonant tone.

There was the time that Gianluigi Buffon opted for '88' when playing for Parma. Not only is it a weird choice for a keeper, the former Italian number one also managed to get himself in hot water because '88' is a prominent neo-Nazi symbol – 'H' being the eighth letter of the alphabet, meaning 88 equates to HH, or Heil Hitler. His defence that instead of any far-right connection, '88' simply reminded him of four balls, a nod to the 'big balls' he would apparently need to get into the Italian squad, was only marginally better.

Or, how about, following in the footsteps of legendary Chelsea strikers Gianluca Vialli, Jimmy Floyd Hasselbaink and Peter Osgood, the season when Steve Sidwell was given the 'No. 9' shirt at Stamford Bridge?

And best of all, there was the occasion when Inter Milan's Ivan Zamorano got around his desire to have the 'No. 9' shirt, which had been nabbed by Ronaldo, by picking No. 18 and planting a + sign in between the numbers. Sadly, what Zamorano failed to realise is that although the sum of 1+8 is indeed nine, it also adds up to 'weird bellend'.

It's now been over two decades since a Premier League team took to the pitch using the first 11 squad numbers, the last outing taking place at Charlton Athletic during the early months of the 1998/99 season.

It's unlikely that any will ever do so again.

Long before Edgar Davids rolled into Barnet, the old familiarities of the 1–11 were already consigned to the past. His moment of unconstrained egotism merely represented the final nail in the coffin.

Deadline Day

Back in the pre-Sky age, ClubCall catered for all your transfer deadline day needs. For the price of a phone call, one that would roughly equal the national debt of a small country, you could learn the exciting news that Mike Milligan had joined your club.

But then Sky came along and changed all that, turning a day of moderate football business into event television.

Deadline Day has become the time when Sky sellotapes down the caps lock and tells us 'ANYTHING IS POSSIBLE'. And technically that's true. Like any given day, anything can occur – Martians could land, the oceans could run dry, the Second Coming might arrive. But, in reality, for much of Deadline Day's history, that 'possible' has mostly just been Harry Redknapp doing some last-minute shopping in the disappointment aisle.

For Sky, the lack of frenetic activity and the scarcity of headline-grabbing moves is a problem. Event television must be fed, a rapacious appetite almost impossible to sate. Rumours, repeat rumours, fake rumours – nothing is off the table. The need for unceasing narratives embraces all as Sky puts its full arsenal to the task, marshalling its resources to find out exactly when Peter Odemwingie hasn't moved to QPR.

Its reporters are cast far and wide, loitering around training grounds and stadiums in the hope of arrivals. For some of these beleaguered souls, it will be an exercise infutility, dispatched on a fool's errand to wait for players that were never going to come.

In a desperate effort to fill the belly of the beast, the broadcaster throws the net wider, turning to its 'citizen reporters'. Across the country, reports fly in on social media, semi-sightings of people who might be footballers: 'Andy Carroll has been seen buying a steak slice from a Greggs in Leeds', 'Enner Valencia is currently wandering around baggage reclaim at Gatwick', 'Wilson Palacios was just spotted playing the fruit machines at Newport Pagnell services'.

Life is particularly tough for Sky in the winter, the more flaccid of the two windows. Its close of business has become a day from which excitement is almost impossible to wring; the chronic lack of activity attributable to the growing realisation that attempting to cram a club's shopping needs into four weeks inevitably creates mistakes. Like a deranged supermarket shopper filling their trolley with whatever is available, ending up with more Fray Bentos pies than any human could stomach, clubs have been stung too many times before. That's how you end up with Cenk Tosun, that most 'Fray Bentos' of footballers.

But winter or summer, the whole thing, the endless lies, the yellow colour coordination, the cash totaliser, might all be just about bearable if Sky acknowledged the paucity of its material; if the rumours were treated proportionately. But instead, the broadcaster's hyperbole machine whirls into full effect, treating every titbit like earth-shattering news.

It makes you wonder how Sky Sports would report something that was truly 'earth-shattering'. Picturing a winged Jim White, his eyes wild, hair aflame, dressed in golden robes, the living embodiment of Ossa, the Greek God of News. From his jewelled trumpet, Jim would blast the headlines into the very souls of those watching at home, a searing pulse of information that would leave its recipients momentarily bewildered.

Come to think of it, that might actually be worth tuning in to.

Diving

Their commitment is absolute. Employing the Stanislavski system of method acting, they inhabit the role for weeks beforehand; falling to the ground under the slightest of touches around the family home, pretending to be shot in the back by a sniper while out doing the big Friday shop, generally acting like a bit of a pr**k wherever possible. And then, come game time, they're centred and ready, just waiting for that key moment in the box, the slightest of nudges or the grazing of a trailing leg and down they go, a moment of pure acting perfection.

As with any occurrence like this, inevitably, it reawakens the debate around diving, and specifically the contention that it's ruining football.

Seen very much as a modern disease, barely a week goes by without an incident of simulation making headlines. Some players, such as Raheem Sterling, Mo Salah and Harry Kane have indulged so frequently that a reputation has built around them, the label 'serial diver' hanging over their heads in shame.

For a long time, pundits of a certain age (who always seem to look and sound suspiciously like Graeme Souness) have labelled this a 'foreign' disease, brought to these shores by an invading horde, whose casual morality and inherent lack of basic British decency gives them the flexibility to practise the footballing dark arts.

But considering the breakneck speed with which domestic players bought into the allure of diving, it's fair to say that even if it ever was an entirely foreign-born concept, once introduced, British players became as adept as any at simulating contact.

Although such instances have long been punishable by a yellow card, a few years ago, in response to another media outcry at diving's prevalence, the FA brought in a new offence, grandly titled 'Successful Deception of a Match Official'. Under this, a player could be retrospectively punished if a match official had been deceived by an act of simulation, and as a direct result, the offending player's team had been awarded a penalty and/or an opposing player dismissed.

Only a handful of players have ever been punished and, unsurprisingly, none from the elite teams (within whose ranks the serial offenders often reside).

Like a Year 11 bully punching down rather than up, keen to flex his muscles but too frightened to take on the sixth formers, the FA confined their actions to the likes of Morecambe (Sam Lavelle), West Brom (Dwight Gayle) and Leeds United (Patrick Bamford).

Having made their point, but importantly not offended the Premier League big boys, the new sanction lingers on the statute book but is rarely exercised.

So, simulation continues to mar the game. But for every cloud there's always a silver lining and with diving that has to be the impact it's all having on Souness, a man whose mind seems to be buckling under the strain of it all. There's a large vein on his forehead that appears to be on the verge of popping and we're probably only one dive away, likely from a foreign player, from poor old Graeme losing it altogether. Come on Salah, you can do it!

Dodgy Handballs

Ever since football diverged from rugby in the 1860s, leaving that sport to the unlikely alliance of public school boys and woollybacks, the game has had a handball rule. And, until recently, the key deciding factor in the offence was intention. If a player was judged to have deliberately handled the ball, then a free kick or penalty was given, depending where on the pitch the offence took place.

But concerned that a rule that was fully understood and had functioned perfectly well for over a century might be too vague, the International Football Association Board (IFAB), the body that determines the laws of the game, recently decided to have a tinker, reforming handball to essentially take intent out of the equation.

Like the introduction of VAR, the redefinition forms part of the modern game's obsession with the penalty kick and the desire to ensure that every possible one must be awarded. Those fuelling this fetishisation believe that a plethora of micro-transgressions, unseen handballs and fouls have long been robbing the football world of the penalties it so richly deserves.

With the new interpretation and an arsenal of camera angles in support, this great wrong can finally be addressed. Under the new reality, a player in the box can now be punished for the crime of loitering near a football while in possession of arms. The player doesn't even need to be looking at the ball or even be aware of where it is. It just needs to hit them. The redefinition has allowed referees to judge almost any contact with the hand/arm in the box as a foul and at last satisfy the sport's palpable desire for more spot kicks.

And, as an added bonus it has also encouraged the spread of the modern phenomenon known as the 'Michael Flatley' defensive shape, which has seen modern defenders adopt a 'Lord of the Dance' pose while trying to jockey attacking players, their arms glued to their sides, legs working frenetically, all the time attempting to ensure that a stray ricochet doesn't strike them on the arm.

Inevitably, much to the football world's relief, the creation of this new system of rules and interpretation has made things much clearer for everyone involved. Finally, after 160 long years, English football is at last free of controversy when it comes to handball. Which means the IFAB has got the spare time to look at other parts of the game crying out for reform. Now, about that offside rule …

Adrian Durham

The worst thing to happen to radio since Lord Haw Haw, Adrian Durham was once described by *The Guardian* as 'an expert phone-in troll. Arrogantly spouting inflammatory football opinions, in the hope of prompting some indignant phone rage from an uppity fan.' Like all self-defined 'shock jocks', Durham trades in the deliberately provocative, staking out hopelessly indefensible positions in the hope that enough enraged people with too much time on their hands can phone in and soak up the inordinate amount of broadcast hours that TalkSport has to fill.

Durham helms the station's coveted drivetime show, where he's joined by a sentient Toby jug called Darren Gough. While Durham goads the listening public, Gough chortles supportively, occasionally chipping in with the kind of expert football analysis that can only truly be gained by playing cricket professionally.

In many ways Durham's approach is a symptom of a struggle that lies at the heart of TalkSport, a station that finds itself caught between two worlds. On the one hand it has tried, with some success, to operate as a genuine, quality alternative to 5Live, investing heavily in its live coverage. We're a long way from the days, not too long ago, when it made up for its lack of live football rights by commentating on games on the TV and piping in crowd noise.

But on the other hand, it still remains tethered to the spirit of its founder, Abaddon the Defiler, the entity who slithered into our dimension many years ago, possessing the bloated carcass of a recently deceased middle-aged man and taking on a new identity: Kelvin MacKenzie.

Abaddon has forged a career on two guiding principles: to provoke where possible and to appeal to mankind's worst impulses. That's how he ended up at *The Sun*, the manifestation of everything we hate about ourselves (plus trips to Calais for £1).

He founded TalkSport back in 1999, encouraging that lust for controversy to permeate the station's culture. Since he left in 2005, returning to print media in pursuit of 'The Truth', the station has slowly tried to rid itself of its founder's principles. But despite progress, it still at times feels like an aural rendition of *The Sun*'s back pages, none more so than when Durham is at the mic.

The only way to negate his deliberately provocative approach would be non-response. Stripped of the oxygen that the outraged public provide, he would be left bereft, just him and his little Toby jug, vast hours to fill and nothing to fill them with. Which sounds like a better idea for a show.

Endorsements

Picture Michael Owen, sat at the helm of his helicopter simulator, a filmed airstrip backdrop scrolling behind, his vacant eyes staring down the camera lens. Without enthusiasm or warmth, he asks you to come to 'see Dubai'. In that second, you briefly wonder how this idea ever got past the pitch stage. And then you remember cocaine. Because surely only a marketing team nose deep in the stuff could ever have dreamed up and sanctioned anything as horrifying as this.

Owen, who in terms of screen presence is outshone throughout by the inanimate control stick that he wields during this ten-minute visual atrocity, is a man of singular delivery. Irrespective of the emotion being expected, he'll provide you with the same robotic cadence, displaying the kind of consistency he once showed in front of goal before his hamstrings melted.

As an advert, it works best for locations other than Dubai because it convinces you wholeheartedly that any place on earth that this man enjoys visiting can't be a place you would want to be.

Although a harrowing example, Owen's Dubai misadventure is just one part of a growing trend that has seen modern footballers increasingly whore out their image to the highest bidder. In the modern game, nothing is off the table. In recent years, if you wanted to flog things as diverse as *X-Men Apocalypse,* Japanese facial cream and chicken processing, footballers, in the guise of Wayne Rooney, Lionel Messi and the entire Blackburn Rovers squad respectively, have been on hand to help.

Of course, almost as long as there have been professional players, there have been businesses trying to make a few quid off them. At the height of his powers in the 1930s, Dixie Dean helped flog Carreras cigarettes ('the cigarettes with a kick in them'). But when you don't earn much more than the punters on the terraces, such a move was understandable.

The same isn't true for modern footballers. While their career might have a similar shelf life, for the players at the top, those who most regularly hawk themselves out, the money is nowhere near as comparable. Elite-level players can now comfortably earn enough cash in a few seasons to see them out for the rest of their days. The financial imperative to prostitute their image is losing its compulsion.

But that doesn't stop them. Take Cristiano Ronaldo, who last year earned around £35m from endorsements. While many of his current and past corporate relationships have a sporting/athletic connection, the majority don't, and in recent years he's lent his image to an eclectic mix, including the likes of Egyptian Steel, Panzer Glass and Tag Heuer.

Now, I could be doing Cristiano a disservice. For all I know he might well be a huge fan of smelting, so, for him, the relationship with Egyptian Steel was a lifelong dream come true. But I'm probably not.

Although, you have to give Egyptian Steel credit. With his winning smile and magnetic charisma, you can see why they went with Ronaldo. Apparently, they learned a valuable lesson from neighbouring Libya, whose own steel industry opted for Michael Owen. With his self-penned catchphrase 'I like steel', and a screen presence that illuminated the world like the dying embers of a discarded cigarette, it took mere weeks for the Libyan steel industry to go into terminal decline.

Eng-ger-land Mania

So many of us look back on USA 1994 with a sense of warm nostalgia. Diana Ross missing a sitter during the opening ceremony, John Aldridge's expletive-laden bollocking of a touchline official, Alexi Lalas and Roberto Baggio competing to win the mantle of the tournament's s**ttest barnet. But perhaps most of all we view USA 1994 fondly because England were nowhere near it.

After failing to qualify, the first time that had happened since 1978, a generation of fans got to experience what it was like to watch a World Cup free from the curse that's

Eng-ger-land. No scenes of topless, heavily paunched, paralytic fans rampaging through American streets and no Union Jack flags at games, each emblazoned with a name drawn from the list of middle England's exotic towns: Yate, Corby, Nuneaton!

But perhaps best of all, no chance of Eng-ger-land mania at home. It takes very little for Eng-ger-land mania to grip the nation. Even in the modern game, when successive footballing disappointments have supposedly given this country a functioning sense of proportion, as soon as the faintest hint of success rears its head, the mania begins to stir.

Suddenly, the back pages begin to beat their jingoistic jungle drums, extolling us to get behind 'Our Boys'.

As kick-off nears, giant screens in town centres start to attract fans in their thousands, drawn to their siren song. Collectively, their passion is irrepressible. For many infected with Eng-ger-land mania, it doesn't matter that just weeks ago few cared for the progress of this team. Suddenly, its success or failure is a matter of life or death.

For those indifferent to the national team, almost in the blink of an eye, you become outsiders, cast into social Siberia. There's an in-group and an out-group. Those who love their country and those who apparently hate it. Those who throw their pints into the air and those who drink them.

And the further England progress, the greater the in-group becomes, swelling exponentially, an amorphous mass of tight-fitting polo shirts, excessive hair product and evocations of the Dunkirk spirit.

But within its body, the seeds of its own destruction have long since been sown. Because this is an England crowd, not a German crowd. Failure is written into its DNA. Inevitably, at some point before the final, the team will conspire to balls things up, leaving a nation crestfallen.

And then life moves on. The town centres fall quiet, no more pints to be thrown in joy. Eng-ger-land mania never lasts beyond tournaments, interest in the national team switching almost without a breath to indifference amongst most. But even in the lulls, you know it's just waiting, biding its time for the next occasion when England scrape through the group stage of an international tournament, ready to unleash itself on the country once again.

The Engländ Band

Terry Venables has done two unforgivable things in his life. First, in 2002, together with the inconsequential boy band Rider, he recorded 'England Crazy', a calamity of a song, so torturous that it still remains prohibited under Article 3 of the Geneva Convention.

And secondly, perhaps more damningly, he was instrumental in the creation of the England Band in 1996, a decision for which he should probably have his playing and managerial record in this country expunged from the record books as punishment.

Back then, in their first guise, the men behind this were known as the Sheffield Wednesday Kop Band, a group of fans who would belt out brass renditions of Owls terrace favourites during home games.

But following Venables and the FA's invitation to recreate for the national team what they were doing at Hillsborough, everything changed. Their singular approach to the fan experience was elevated to a national level. It turned what had been very much just a Hillsborough problem into something we all had to endure now.

The England Band, essentially drums, trumpet and a euphonium, boast a repertoire that's exceptionally narrow, largely comprising endless renditions of 'Rule Britannia', 'God Save the Queen' (sadly, not the Sex Pistols version) and the theme from *The Great Escape*. It might be the case that when, as youngsters, they were mastering their instruments, their parents inadvertently looked up prospective tutors in the Racist Yellow Pages.

Another depressing aspect of their continued existence is the sheer constancy of their music. The band don't react, bursting into song at moments of high drama. Instead, they provide a continuous musical backdrop, a constant drone, which smothers what little joy a typical England performance provides.

The strangest aspect about the longevity of the England Band is the fact that nobody seems to like them. Even England supporters aren't keen, a demographic for whom the band's musical aesthetic – an England of village greens, warm beer and Imperial preference – seems ready made.

But, perhaps worst of all is the thought that there might be no end to this torture. Back in 2012, the band was refused entry to England's first game of the Euros in Donetsk, even suffering the shame of having their instruments confiscated by security officials. Here, at last, was the opportunity we had all waited for, a chance for the FA to hang them out to dry and wash their hands of the debacle once and for all. But they couldn't even get that right, lobbying on behalf of the band to ensure that they were back, instruments in hand, for the next game.

It seems as though as long as they have air in their lungs, the England Band will continue, their monotonous dirge in many ways the perfect encapsulation of the England international football experience.

English Jobs for English Managers

With gammonish fury, the cry bellows out: 'Where are all the English managers?' 'Where have they gone?' They search high and low, looking for their countrymen, those stout-hearted, no-nonsense, yeoman of old. What they find disappoints. Johnny Foreigner, with his good looks, his innate sophistication and his progressive attitude towards diet is everywhere.

They've come over here and taken our jobs, the lament goes. These are English jobs for English managers.

They rail against one of the positives of the Premier League, its increasingly internationalist perspective. From being a game that was once dominated by players and managers drawn from the home nations, the country's elite division is now one that draws the brightest and best from across the world.

But for a residual, yet vocal and persistent minority, this trend has been an affront to everything that's right and proper. With depressing regularity, they're wheeled out to spout their reactionary views, moaning at length at the restriction of opportunities for local lads to have a crack at the top jobs.

Why, they argue, hasn't the job of delivering thrilling attacking football at Manchester United been given to Sam Allardyce? How come, they ask, elite clubs aren't clamouring to appoint Alan Pardew following his death spiral at West Brom? And why is it, they inquire, that Tony Pulis, originator of the back ten formation, can no longer get a job in the country's top division?

It's a foreign bias, they mumble, arguing that if a young English manager like Sean Dyche were to change his name to Sean Dycheo, he would be in charge of a top six club in a heartbeat. It's a perspective that significantly underestimates the care and attention that elite clubs put into recruitment, assuming that the addition of a letter 'O' would somehow confound them enough into believing that the pallid, ginger-goateed, gravel-voiced man in front of them was not, in fact, Sean Dyche.

It's hard not to read into these demands an undercurrent of xenophobia, a lingering hostility to those from other countries who have taken something that the 'England for the English' brigade regard as their own, a sense of self-entitlement based on nothing more than geography.

It's this feeling of ownership that clouds any acknowledgement that maybe it's the shortcomings of those they propose that's holding them back. That perhaps owners who have invested millions into their clubs don't really want to see their expensively assembled team stick ten behind the ball in the hope of grinding out a draw.

But, despite this lack of introspection, these views remain part of the game. They, like the frothed bile of Nigel Farage, the continued existence of *The Sun* and inexplicable appeal of little Tommy Robinson, have an audience. And with the chances that England will one day turn into a paradise of tolerance retreating with every *Daily Mail* headline, it seems that until a son of these isles actually lands a job at a big club, they're going to remain with us for some time to come.

The European Super League

Like the Saturday night, prime-time career of Michael McIntyre, it's the terrible idea that won't go away. Rumours have circulated for the past 30 years that dark forces amongst the elite of the game have been conspiring behind the scenes to create what they've long pined for, a new European Super League (ESL).

In 2018, leaked documents published by *Der Spiegel* revealed that these machinations are finally beginning to look more concrete.

The documents suggested that elite clubs had met together in a kind of footballing version of the Bilderberg conference, where the game's very own illuminati gathered to carve up the future of sport, devise new ways to take a greater share of revenues and probably sacrifice the occasional goat or two.

They put together a plan that would see the creation of a league of up to 18 European teams, made up of those with the strongest television presence.

The envisaged competition would involve 11 of Europe's biggest clubs, pretentiously known as the 'founders', along with a number of initial 'guests'. In a boon for those who love their football to be as tedious as possible, the so-called founders, including Manchester United, Chelsea and Liverpool, wouldn't face relegation and would be guaranteed membership for 20 years.

It represented just one of several plans that have circulated in recent years, each characterised by the same sense of elite clubs pulling away, yanking up the drawbridge and gorging on the riches of the game.

Even if you're entirely comfortable with naked avarice, the impact on the domestic league structure left behind should worry anyone who values the integrity of the football pyramid. Because, although not immediately, but certainly over the course of a few decades, the ESL would syphon off supporters and revenue, in much the same way as Premier League has done to the Football League below for the past 30 years, hollowing out so much of our national game in the process.

Not that the elite will care of course. For them, it all makes perfect sense. Their dream is to live in a world in which the Spanish support Real Madrid or Barcelona, the English Manchester United, Chelsea or Liverpool, the Germans Dortmund or Bayern, and so on. It's not about sport, it's about market dominance.

It's best not to think of elite teams as football clubs. Because they're not. They might dress themselves up in more humble clothing and bandy around terms like 'tradition' and 'community', but these are businesses, and ones that are as laser-focused on the bottom line and free from moral considerations as the worst kind of hedge fund.

The ESL will be their crowning glory, the pinnacle of a trend that has been years in the making. The final victory for those who believe that football without money, not fans, is nothing.

The FA

Where to begin? Possibly with the FA's supine capitulation to the Premier League in the governance of the top flight? Or maybe the way in which the self-proclaimed guardians of the grassroots game have spent the last few decades being anything but? And how about the numerous occasions it has become embroiled in scandals involving racism, homophobia and sexism?

And all of this before you even get to the FA's make-up at the highest level; an institution so male, old and white it makes the Conservative Party look like the Black Panthers.

Almost as long as there has been organised football in England, there has been the FA, founded by a handful of public school old-boys back in 1863. And since then, its attitude has remained rooted in the traditions of England's fee-paying schools, a kind of deep-seated conservatism, hostile to change and anything that whiffs of modernity.

The 20th century, in particular, wasn't the FA's finest hour. Banning women from playing, leaving racism in the game unchecked, failing to implement even the most basic of safeguarding standards in youth football. If there was a mistake to make, the FA would make it.

Since then, often against its will, the organisation has been dragged kicking and screaming into the 21st century. But, despite its modern veneer, you still get the sense that at heart the FA seems to position itself around 20-odd years behind societal trends. So, right now, for them, it's still the late 1990s, meaning that along with it being okay to tolerate casual racism and 'banter' misogyny, they're still really into Britpop and Tamagotchi.

Along with an inability to move with the times, over the years the FA has also acquired a reputation for administrative failure, such as the massively over-budget new national stadium and the way in which it has mismanaged grassroots football. If the organisation excels at anything, it seems to be at cocking up.

Depressingly, despite the FA's continuous missteps, by merit of very occasionally getting some things right, it seems to do just enough to resist calls for the whole organisation to be wound up and replaced by something more fitting for the game today.

But should that be the case? Just because an organisation is occasionally competent or intermittently progressive, should it be beyond criticism or deserve to be a central part of England's footballing landscape? After all, you don't forgive the horrors of Nazi Germany simply because Hitler could knock out a decent motorway and had a forward-thinking approach towards woodland conservation.

Back when the FA was founded in the 1860s, a lot of the things that were tolerated in those days seem strange to our modern eyes. Things like sending kids up chimneys, denying women the vote and getting the Chinese hooked on opium being a legitimate part of British foreign policy. We don't do any of those things anymore, but we do still tolerate the FA.

It's an organisation that should have been put out of its misery years ago. A few 4G pitches and a commercial partnership with Pokémon doesn't change that fact.

Even English football deserves better.

Fan TV

We have a lot to thank the internet for: greater interconnectivity, the democratisation of information, cat memes. But nothing is ever perfect and, along with the above, it has also brought us other, less welcome developments, such as cyberbullying, the death of privacy and those 'inspirational' quotes that your mum puts on Facebook.

Fan TV, the humble fanzine repurposed for the digital age, is one of those online developments that seems to have a foot in each camp. When done well, it can provide a voice for fans and offer a more authentic and better-informed alternative to the national media.

But when done badly, it's just s**te.

Part of the problem with Fan TV is the immediacy of the medium. In the literary days of the past, a time when the only way to vent your anger at a club was the fanzine, the time delay gave room for consideration. That knee-jerk, post-match response was allowed time to ebb. Not so with Fan TV, where instant accessibility and demand for immediate content discards the lost art of reflection.

All those unpleasant, poorly thought out opinions, the kind that the match can so easily conjure up, now have a medium where they can be expressed freely. And because anyone, in theory, can get on camera, you sometimes end up giving a platform to the kind of supporters who should probably never be let anywhere near a camera. In the past, such fans might have been confined to hectoring unwilling listeners that had been trapped on their way to the toilets in the pub after the game. But with Fan TV, their signature brand of unedited horses**t is given the room to reach a much wider audience.

Not that those who run some of these channels seem to mind. Many live and die by the number of subscribers they bring in, as that represents the best way that content can be monetised. And nothing sells like a dickhead. In expressing the kind of half-arsed, back-of-a-fag-packet analysis beloved of some channels, they can be guaranteed plenty of traction on the 'socials' and, in turn, ever swelling subscribers.

But, as bad as this is, even that's preferable to the other path that some take to grow numbers, the decision to turn from poacher to gamekeeper. While controversy might bring in the punters, it pales in comparison to the clinching of interviews with players and coaches. There's always something undeniably sad when a fan channel makes the switch, selling its soul for access. You watch as anything considered 'off brand' slowly slips away, the medium turning bit by bit into just another mouthpiece for the club. And when that happens, you're left with an empty shell, a desiccated husk where vibrancy used to be.

Or, as it's otherwise known, *The Anfield Wrap.*

Fantasy Football

Who Ate All Depays? Lallanas in Pyjamas, Benteke Fried Chicken; the puns alone should probably be enough to damn fantasy football forever.

There was a time when such names were consigned to the world of five-a-side, with only hundreds of thousands exposed to their crapness. With the ever-expanding millions now playing FPL, the suffering is so much greater.

Then there's the reality of the game itself. Football is by its very nature a partisan sport, one defined as much by our hatred of others as it is by the love of our own. But when it comes to fantasy football, all that goes out the window. You might be a devout Gunner but go big on Spurs because the 'metrics' suggest a hefty points haul. When you find yourself getting a quick thrill because a player you hate, playing for a team you hate, just got an assist, it's probably time to take a good, long look at yourself.

Of course, there *are* purists, those who refuse to adopt players from loathed rivals – United fans who forgo Agüero, Gunners who say no to Kane. But they're a rare few. Far more common instead for FPL to suck you into its vortex of partisan-free football, where tolerance and appreciation of talent, irrespective of club, replace bitterness and hostility, the norms of the game that have long made it the truly beautiful sport it is.

But there's more. My cousin, a man who doesn't really know anything about football, won the 2015/16 FPL league I was in. His technique of just picking the few players he had heard of proved far more effective than my studiously researched approach. And to rub salt into the wound, he won it with a team called Tea and Busquets, the worst of all puns (not that it still bothers me).

His success didn't just prove that skill means little in the game, it also made a mockery of the expert/pundit sideshow that has sprung up around fantasy football in recent years. Newspaper columns, podcasts, entire magazines and websites devoted to the art, a whole side industry providing in-depth analysis for a game that's essentially based on luck (again, I'm over it).

But if you want final definitive proof that the whole thing is just a waste of time, it's this: back in 2008/09, if you didn't have Stephen Ireland in your team from the beginning of the season, you had no chance of doing well. That's Stephen Ireland. On that point alone, I rest my case.

FIFA 21

Tricks, skillz, goals, signature celebrations, superstar players, more goals, elite teams, the Champions League, even more goals, 'bantz', tekkers ... and did I mention the goals?

FIFA is the jewel in EA Sports' gaming crown. And it's one that's restlessly seeking authenticity. Matt Prior,

FIFA's current creative director, has said, 'Until FIFA is indistinguishable from football in real life and plays exactly like football, we'll always have more to do.' The assumption being that FIFA is playing catch-up.

But I think Matt's got it the wrong way around. FIFA is football's future. It's the real-life game that's doing the catching up.

The obsession with the big brand clubs, players who are more style than substance, an inexorable sense of momentum moving towards larger and larger scorelines; increasingly football is being shaped to cater for an audience incapable of concentrating for long periods and who need razzmatazz on a regular basis. It's the FIFA generation, a great swathe of the football-watching population whose perspective on the game has been shaped by EA.

When you're playing a 12-minute game that's jam-packed with incidents and showered with 'tekkers', it's understandable that watching Burnley and Sheffield United grind out a 0-0 draw might pale by comparison. FIFA isn't a game where caution and organisation is commonly seen or appreciated (which might be why I can't get out of Division 8 in Ultimate Team).

At least in the past video games had the decency to be a bit s**t. 'Match Day' on the ZX Spectrum, 'Elite Soccer' on the SNES, 'Sensible Soccer' on the Amiga, were games so far removed from real-life football that you could never, for a moment, believe that what you were playing was anything other than a crap, virtual form of the game. 'Elite Soccer', in particular, had an infuriating glitch where the goalkeepers would occasionally just stop playing. Some people believe

Loris Karius's Champions League Final performance against Real Madrid in 2018 paid homage to this.

The impact of these games on the wider footballing world was negligible. They didn't shape our understanding of football or change what we expected from it. Just because it was possible to run away from the referee to escape a yellow card when playing 'Match Day', didn't mean we wanted that to be replicated on a Saturday afternoon. Although, thinking about it, watching Mike Dean chasing Fabian Delph around the pitch, card held aloft, might not be that bad a thing.

But FIFA is different. More immersive and much more realistic, it's warping what its players expect from Football 1.0. And the physical game is responding, as it attempts to maintain the attention of an audience that's increasingly uninterested in the less glamorous aspects of the sport.

We're all gamers now. The FIFA-isation of football is here to stay.

Formations

Will Liverpool line up in a 3-4-3? How will United cope with Manchester City's inverted full-backs? Has 3-5-2 replaced 4-2-3-1?

Consider this – despite the wide array of formations and tactics available in the English game, the innovations that are taking place season by season, it's still the same handful of clubs that reside at the top each year.

So far, there has been no magic formula, no undiscovered formation or tactic to change that reality in any meaningful or long-lasting way. With depressing accuracy, what determines the shape and structure of football in this country is money.

The bigger your budget, by and large, the higher you'll finish.

Spennymoor Town aren't going to scale the heights of the English pyramid just because their manager has discovered a new way of playing with two at the back.

It seems that the days when innovators were able to crash into the elite through footballing innovation alone have largely gone. Modern football's venerated paradigm shifters, coaches like Guardiola and Klopp, always do their 'innovation' at the highest levels, armed to the teeth with overly generous transfer budgets.

For a lot of the time, when we analyse tactics and formations, it's like looking back through history when heavily weaponised European powers took on indigenous tribes, the latter often armed with little more than a few spears and a can-do attitude. In the wake of the inevitable victory for the visitors, you could praise the way the invading Europeans set up, the tactics and impressive show of organisation, but let's face it, they could have blundered into battle pissed, blindfolded and with one hand tied behind their backs, and still pulled off an away win.

Perhaps, when it comes to formations, there might be a better way of displaying the teams before kick-off. Rather than showing the set-up and then having the pundits pore over the possible tactics in detail, Sky should just flag up how much each team has cost to assemble.

Will Manchester United (£700m) get the better of Burnley (£80m)? Do Newcastle United (£120m) have what it takes to overcome Manchester City (£780m)?

You could even make it more interesting for those watching at home by having a running total of the players' values floating above their heads as they run around the pitch. So, when Alex Iwobi is on the bench, a figure of £20m might be above him. Then, after he comes on, we can watch as it drops by the second with every poorly placed pass and positional mistake.

Gareth Southgate – England Manager

Deep in the heart of St George's Park, FA scientists have spent years toiling away, a decades-long quest to find the magic formula that would allow them to create the perfect specimen.

And then, in 2016, a breakthrough! Finally, through the successful melding of man, blazers and FA instructional manual, a new species was born: Homo-FAamus.

Bland, pliable and imbued with the air of substitute geography teacher, they gave this new creation a human name: Gareth Southgate. And he has proven to be everything they ever wanted.

In the past, the FA has been burdened by managers that came with their own ideas and fallibilities. Managers who would make terrible claims about society's disabled citizens, who would be open to corruption, who would play Steve Guppy at left wing-back. But no more.

Fully versed in FA theology, Southgate has been the perfect medium to obediently initiate the organisation's long-term plan to reshape the national footballing character, for it to mirror the world champions. Not the current world champions, of course. Or the ones before that. Because that would make too much sense. Instead, the FA is taking the country forward into a brave new footballing world by turning the clock back to 2010.

English teams must now dominate possession and try wherever possible to emulate the Spanish world champions of a decade ago. Only, they'll do this with an English spin, one that puts the emphasis on dour, pointless possession and a crab-like adherence to sideways passing. Forward momentum must always be left to the opposition.

Who cares that English centre-halves, with first touches that are basically tackles, have about as much chance at mastering possession football as Eric Dier does of getting a job as a matchday steward? Or that the game has moved on, Tiki-taka blown away in a blitzkrieg of Teutonic heavy metal football? It will become the way we do things, FA dogma gradually constraining the national team, in the process suffocating some of the most exciting attacking talent the country has ever produced.

And Homo-FAamus will be the standard bearer, a man loyal to the cause. Through the power of waistcoats, unerring politeness and Mason Mount, this product of St George's Park will captain the starship FA on its long-term mission to explore strange new opponents, to seek out new life and new civilisations, to boldly go where the Spanish have sort of gone before.

Glory Hunters

For much of football's long history, two factors dictated the team you followed: family and geography. And that was it. If the footballing gods weren't on your side, placing perennial under-achievers in the city you were born, or within the bounds of your family, then that was too bad.

But in the modern game, those certainties are being eroded as the main brands have begun to pull in supporters from across the country at an unprecedented rate.

A third of Manchester United's domestic supporters now come from southern England. More people in London support Liverpool than the number that support the club in Liverpool itself. It seems that those old determinants of loyalty aren't as strong as they used to be.

Football has become a commodity and, as consumers, many fans are looking for good value in their support. It's no longer about community and tradition but instead about 'bang for your buck'. If you're going to invest in a club, financially and emotionally, it seems that getting a guaranteed return now plays a part. And that means choosing a big club.

Why support Millwall when you can support Liverpool? Why endure the constant frustration of following Gillingham when becoming a Manchester United fan can offer so much more?

The growth and normalisation of this kind of approach to fandom, of choosing your team by looking at the table and not a map, has even encouraged the proliferation of a once reviled form of supporter: the 'switcher'.

In the past these figures were rare, examples rightly shunned by polite society. I can recall, as a kid, that my dad refused to return to see his very competent dentist after he discovered this boyhood Evertonian had switched allegiances to Liverpool, such was the stain on his character that this transition revealed.

And yet, perhaps emboldened by wider changes in the game, they've become more common of late. Before the start of the 2015/16 season, a survey into the Premier League found that one in ten of its fans were going to switch their allegiances to a new team before a ball had been kicked.

It seems that for a new generation of supporters, the prospect of a lifetime of drudgery, crushing disappointment and a palpable sense of misery no longer holds quite the appeal that it once did.

Goal Music

Imagine your team has just scored. You're instantly filled with happiness, precipitating an emotional outpouring unlike anything that you'll experience in the course of a normal week. It's the reason why you go to watch football. That moment of unadulterated joy.

And then you hear 'Rockin' All Over the World' by Status Quo blast out over the tannoy, the opening bars of jaunty piano a prelude to the 'boogie rock' horror to follow. As the Quo's three chords march their way around the stadium, repetitively stamping out all joy in their wake, they bring with them Francis Rossi's impassioned lyrics. He's a man possessed, insistent on the need to be a-rockin'.

In the blink of an eye, your happiness has evaporated. In that moment, 'Goal Music' has worked its special magic.

During the course of an average football match, the one event guaranteed to make the crowd erupt in full voice is a goal. At no time in football's long history has a goal been met with complete indifference. It's the point of the game. But for some clubs, that's not enough. For them, this spontaneous eruption of ecstasy must now have a musical accompaniment. Goal music, the fever dream of an over-promoted marketing executive, has now become a fact of life.

Common across Continental Europe, songs vary from club to club. But whatever is chosen, each one leans towards the up-tempo. We're yet to see a goal be accompanied by something from Leonard Cohen's vast back catalogue.

The Bundesliga stands as Europe's main offender, with the likes of Werder Bremen – '500 Miles' (The Proclaimers), RB Leipzig – 'I Feel Good' (James Brown) and Borussia Mönchengladbach – 'Maria I Like it Loud' (Scooter), vying for the title of the division's worst.

But even the Germans don't come close to the monstrosity unleashed on the world by Ligue 1's Lille. Clearly believing that Blur's 'Song 2' lacked the required punch, inspiration struck. Moments before Graham Coxon's scuzzy guitar kicks in, they inserted the wild screams of Fred Flintstone's 'Yabba Dabba Doo!' Lille's fans must be that rarest of things in football, supporters who yearn for a goalless draw.

In England, the spread of this disease is only in its early stages, with sporadic instances confined to a handful of sufferers, such as Wigan Athletic and Norwich City. But the infection might not remain mild for much longer. During the coronavirus pandemic, several clubs used the absence of crowds as an opportunity to sneak goal music into their stadiums, safe in the knowledge that they would be insulated from the rage it would cause amongst fans. You get the feeling that people who run our clubs are just itching to ensure that every goal that takes place will one day be accompanied by a snippet of up-tempo musical hell.

Goals, Goals, GOALS!!!!!

6-0 Boom! 7-2 Kaboom! 9-4 Kablammo! In the heads of those who govern and broadcast the game, this is how football needs to be played; a throw-caution-to-the-wind display of attacking verve.

Since football morphed into an entertainment 'product', one beamed around the world to viewers who often have no emotional involvement in what they're watching, the desire for more goals to be scored has become palpable.

For the Premier League and broadcasters such as Sky and BT, football is now akin to the film industry. And what those responsible for running and televising the game want are blockbusters; big, spectacular, easy to digest visual events, which in the absence of emotional pull, will keep that ever-expanding armchair audience engaged. And 'goals' is how you do that. They're the equivalent of the giant motion-captured Andy Serkis gorilla.

Staying within the same medium, what people like Sky don't want is a low-budget, *Guardian*-acclaimed, indie film. The kind that might be in a foreign language and deal with complex emotional and social issues, like a film about Syrian refugees or family breakdown in rural Croatia. For them, that's what a tightly fought, relatively incident-free 0-0 is. It might be well crafted, riven with subtext and expertly put together, but it's not something that the average punter wants to watch.

And because of this, slowly the game is being augmented to favour attacking football. Over the past 30 years, alterations to the back-pass law, the judgement of offside, and the way in which referees interpret contact have gradually given forwards more protection and greater opportunities to score.

But despite the changes, it's not enough. Frustratingly for those in charge, goals per game remain resolutely on the low side. In the English top flight, they've only increased on average from 2.61 per game two decades ago to around 2.75 today. It's a poor return that's mirrored elsewhere in Europe. Inevitably, in response, greater change is sought.

Already, Arsène Wenger, in his role as FIFA's head of global development, has pressed for the alteration of the offside rule to state that a player will be judged onside if any part of their body that can score a goal is behind or level with the relevant defender. While that same organisation's former technical director Marco van Basten went further, floating the idea of scrapping offside altogether, putting together proposals that effectively read like a goal-hangers' charter.

But who is there to advocate for the tightly fought war of attrition? Where's the counterbalance amongst this drive for cricket scorelines? The game is crying out for someone to speak up for anti-football, a challenge to the likes of Wenger and Van Basten, two men far too wedded to the attacking arts to ever value the darker side of the game.

If FIFA were ever to consider a plurality of opinions, I have the perfect candidate: none other than George Graham. Who better to represent the cause of dour football than a man who saw anything larger than a 1-0 victory as unnecessary extravagance? He would be perfect. Plus, with his chequered financial history and flexible approach to bungs, in many ways he would make the ideal FIFA employee.

Going Topless

Some of history's greatest philosophers have tried to measure happiness. But so intangible is the emotion that its quantification has proven elusive.

Or at least it had until the IFAB had a crack in 2004. Faced with a growing number of players who were starting to celebrate scoring by whipping their shirts off in a moment of unbridled joy, the IFAB decided to step in.

They reasoned that joy could be measured. And for them, the tipping point, the moment that joy became too much joy was exactly the time when a player had reached for their shirt and decided to bare all.

Keen to put a lid on happiness, the IFAB decided to add a detail to Law 12 relating to 'Fouls and Misconduct', stating:

> A player who removes his jersey after scoring a goal
> will be cautioned for unsporting behaviour.

Their explanation for this amendment came a bit later, when in the same document, under the section 'Additional Instructions for Referees and Assistant Referees', the IFAB wrote:

> Removing one's shirt after scoring is unnecessary
> and players should avoid such excessive displays
> of joy.

Like any massively repressed and emotionally constipated native of this country, I don't particularly like seeing players reveal their chests after scoring. Aside from highlighting my own physical inadequacies, I find such an assured sense of body confidence off-putting. But, to deny their right to do so? Assuming they don't whip off their top to reveal a gigantic swastika or a detailed tattoo of Phil Neville, is it really that much of a problem?

And it's not like the IFAB has ever intervened to address other emotional states. Misery, anger, a debilitating sense of ennui – all these have remained perfectly acceptable and boundless. You can have a full existential crisis on the pitch, a moment in which you question the very meaning of life in response to not getting a corner, and the IFAB offer little more than shrugged indifference. But reveal your chest in celebration? That's taking things too far.

You suspect that when the rule was being drawn up, the men at the IFAB were probably just having a bad week.

Maybe it was after Christmas and they were carrying a bit of holiday weight. Suddenly the sight of Ryan Giggs's wonderfully flat stomach just proved too much.

But they should be kinder to themselves. Everyone knows that a six-pack is virtually impossible for any man over the age of 35. We just have to accept the inevitability of our paunches and let those joy-filled players bare all.

Half Scarves

The very nature of football is one of partisanship. You can't have it both ways.

Only, nowadays, apparently you can. About a decade ago, a new football accessory began to emerge, flogged outside grounds across the country. It was an accessory that appeared to defy football logic. Half scarves, as these knitted abominations became known, are exactly what they sound, two halves of different scarves stitched together, with each half representing that day's opposing teams. It's a Frankenstein-esque amalgamation, one that conversely produces something less than the sum of its parts.

With blithe indifference, these scarves trample across the conventions of the game, no pair-up off limits. Rivals are brought together, generations of enmity dismissed with a few stitches. Manchester City are conjoined with Manchester United, Spurs with Arsenal, Celtic with Rangers. It's the kind of logic that could see their manufacturers one day branch out, uniting other disparate groups. Maybe the world of geopolitics is only a few stitches away from the first Boko Haram/USA half scarf.

For those who see them as a scourge, they represent a cultural marker of a new kind of football punter: 'The Tourist'. Attending for the spectacle alone, devoid of connection to either team, they are, for many supporters, a kind of anti-fan, regarding football as an enjoyable day out rather than an exercise in sadomasochism.

For the 'Tourists', the half scarf is a mere souvenir of their day and not an act of knitted cultural vandalism. Free from the complex entanglements of conventional fans, they have no problem purchasing an item that within its stitching contains an inherent contradiction.

That half scarves have distorted something that was once so intrinsic to traditional supporters only compounds the horror. Scarves used to mean something. In the pre-merchandise age, a time before we were ruthlessly mined for our near-exhaustive demand to wear club-endorsed tat, they represented one of the few ways to illustrate allegiance sartorially. The well-worn club scarf became a treasured item, something that stayed with you over the decades, its colours fading, its edges frayed. That's diminished now, the half scarf openly mocking the reverence with which scarves were once held.

And by ripping apart the convention that divided loyalty or indifference should never be revealed, the half scarf has done something else, something more insidious. It has set a precedent. When people attend games today wearing half-and-half kits, eyesores that have been made not bought, certain fans deliberately creating something for which no conceivable demand could ever be understood, we see the legacy of those cotton monstrosities, their poisonous tendrils reaching further and further into the game.

Heat Maps

They say you can prove anything with statistics. But that really doesn't apply to football. Their use might have proliferated in recent years, with the likes of ProZone and Opta producing an endless stream of data, but so much of the game still remains beyond their reach.

To date, there's still no statistical method to measure the psychological impact of a crunching tackle on a mercurial winger or to what degree the dazzling reflection of Roberto Firmino's teeth provide him with a tactical advantage.

Along with the unquantifiable, there's also the quantifiable-but-pointless. In the rush to measure as much of the game as possible, the reach of statistics has embraced areas that don't really tell us that much. And nowhere is this more apparent than heat maps.

Unhelpfully, these maps, using heat signatures, roughly tell us where a player touched the ball most during the match. Importantly, without a bit more digging, they don't tell us what they did with the ball, just where they were when in possession of it.

A heat map of my average day of writing would show me firmly wedged at my desk, unmoving in my apparent dedication to the job. What it wouldn't reveal is just how much of that time was spent dozing off, eating my own weight in biscuits and indulging in lengthy YouTube odysseys, hours spent down a rabbit hole of old clips from *Dr Who*, highlights from 1970s football and numerous videos illustrating the destructive power of tsunamis.

The thing about statistics and analytics is that it all takes a bit of effort. I'll be honest and say that despite its prevalence in football media, I still don't really 'get' Expected Goals (xG). Nor can I be arsed finding out. And because of that, plus a general lack of analytic-literacy, I don't get to talk or write about it.

But the heat map offers us lazy arses a way in, the chance to appear fully versed in the information revolution without putting in the graft. That's the thing about heat maps: it's not really about information, it's about accessibility, an easily digestible medium for the intellectually lethargic.

Think of them like the filmic cannon of Gerard Butler or the music of Coldplay. Sure, much better alternatives are available, but it all involves so much more work than you want to put in. So why not just sit back, take the easy option and let the beige tones of Chris Martin wash over you?

Hipsters

Do you know what the score was in last season's Belarusian Cup Final? What are your thoughts regarding the role that Viktor Maslov played in the development of zonal marking? And, while you're here, do you regard Luca Toni as a Prima Punta or a Seconda Punta?

If you know any of the answers to the above, then you too could become a football hipster. That's assuming that along with a love of the obscure you also revel in the fact that others lack your expansive knowledge and that you're comfortable becoming a self-elected arbiter of good taste.

Hipsterism represents the refocusing of the natural, inherent 'geekiness' of football supporters. We fans might like to think of ourselves as different to trainspotters or those who indulge in a bit of Dungeons and Dragons, but we're not. In-depth knowledge, a near myopic level of obsession, these are all characteristics of supporters and classic hallmarks of 'geekdom' too. But whereas most of us are content to restrict our nerdiness to our own club and the world it operates within, the hipsters have applied these tools to the unloved and the lesser known.

East German football in the 1970s, Hungarian tactical innovation under Gusztáv Sebes, the Greenlandic Football Championship – their only guiding principle on this odyssey into the obscure appears to be a limitation to those parts of the game that the overwhelming majority have no interest in.

But like their cultural cousins, the 'musos', the kind of people who shun anything remotely popular and who were always into bands before they got famous, hipsters can't help marrying all that wonderful knowledge with a sense of undeniable smugness.

'Don't you know who Bela Guttmann is?' 'I think you mean Trequartista, not Il Mediano', 'Isn't being into Dortmund a bit 2014?'

But rather than be a victim to their unbearable smugness, why not turn the tables and try to unsettle them with the following 'facts' of your own:

'Did you know that TV's Telly Savalas once had trials for Yeovil Town?' 'Were you aware that Nicolae Ceauşescu started out in life as a goalkeeper for Steaua Bucharest?' 'Have you heard about the time when Rinus Michels spent three months as manager of Earth Wind and Fire?'

Okay, so none of that's true. But they won't know. And it's obscure enough to make that slappable look of self-satisfaction just melt away.

Hoolie Lit

There were lots of things to like about the 1970s, like punk, powerful trade unions and Findus Crispy Pancakes. But it wasn't all great music, vibrant left-wing politics and delicious breadcrumbed pockets of processed meat. There were also some less-welcome things knocking around too, like the National Front, glam rock and, in the world of football, the emergence of the worst supporters to ever exist. And amazingly, it wasn't the England Band. Instead, it was those who began to see following a team as a medium for violence.

For what are essentially horrible gobs**tes, 'hooligan' is quite an endearing term, bringing to mind some kind of enchanted Irish sprite rather than a shaven-headed Millwall fan whipping out his Stanley knife. But however magical they sounded, the reality was a stain on English football for over two decades, as rampaging groups of 'firms' used fixtures as an excuse to organise fights against rival fans. Ultimately, through better policing and the fact that it began to cost a small fortune to go to the match, the hooligan largely faded from the game from the 1990s onwards.

But somehow, despite this, a nostalgia for them has emerged in recent years. The stories and reminiscences of those involved have been written down and neatly packaged to cater for this new interest, as fans tired of the anodyne reality of modern football have begun to chase a vicarious thrill from the game's troubled past.

So numerous have these tomes become that they've even created their own literary sub-genre: 'Hoolie Lit'. With titles that range from the obvious, such as *Hooligans*, to the hopefully more abstract *We Hate Humans*, hoolie lit has exploded in popularity, giving those from the likes of the ICF and the Chelsea Headhunters the opportunity to tell their story to a new generation of fans.

Inevitably, they've eventually crossed over into the cinematic world, with a succession of hooligan-themed films churned out over the past few decades. Most of them are cheap and uncheerful, straight to DVD fare, designed for those who fancy a change of pace from films about cockney gangsters or Essex wide-boys trying to become cockney gangsters. But, very occasionally, a bit of money gets behind a project and that's how you end up with something like *Green Street*, unequivocally one of the worst films ever made.

Along with glamorising and revelling in senseless violence, *Green Street* also asks its audience to believe that

Frodo Baggins would cut it as a member of the ICF and Charlie Hunnam, boasting a cockney accent so bad that it makes you re-evaluate Dick Van Dyke's, is an authentic East End hoolie.

On release, the film achieved the impossible. For although many of us would rather not find ourselves face to face with the ICF after a game, we would trade that for an instant if the alternative presented was to sit through all 109 minutes of this cinematic travesty, something that's so much worse than hooliganism itself.

Hyperbole

It's been all Chelsea so far (55 seconds into the match). Is it too early to talk about him as the future of the England team (19-year-old after one good game)? Is this the greatest rivalry in the history of football (two teams that have been vying for the title for a few seasons)?

One of the strange side-effects of top-flight football morphing into an entertainment 'product', is the way in which the Premier League is now packaged and marketed.

It's no longer sufficient to describe the reality of a Premier League season: to tell the world that for every Liverpool v Manchester City, there will be many more Burnley v Sheffield Uniteds. That while it will bring a smile to your face to watch Klopp and Guardiola showing their emotions on the touchline, you'll also have the close-up image of an angry Chris Wilder seared into your nightmares.

Punters are fed a lie, a false promise that tells them to buy into an experience that's consistently thrilling, a white-knuckle footballing ride where boredom, mundanity and florid-faced Yorkshiremen are nowhere to be seen.

Sky are the main offenders, desperate to ensure that the money still rolls in. For decades now, the broadcaster's hyperbole machine has been cranked up to 11, a caps-lock existence where proportionality has long since faded away.

Fixtures imbued with a pre-game sense of drama that reality will never match, urgency with every inflection; the marketing and selling of the league goes on all season, rolling waves of hype washing over its customers.

Inevitably, it has changed how football is talked about, hype perniciously spreading to the world beyond Sky's borders. Consideration and nuance have steadily disappeared from football discourse over the past 20 years, replaced by knee-jerk reactions and an endless search for drama.

That's how you end up with Robbie Savage as a pundit. Savage is hyperbole made flesh; a man who lives in a world forever defined by exclamation points. Everything is 'Disgraceful!' or 'Amazing!', irrespective of whether an extreme has been reached. He must be exhausting to live with, lurching from one polar to the next, decrying a 'Disgraceful!' sandwich he's eating before being soothed by an 'Amazing!' packet of Frazzles.

It makes you pine for football's dim and distant past when sedate men, with clipped BBC accents, would sit behind a microphone and simply explain what was happening. It was a hyperbole-free existence, where the most abysmal of performances was merely a 'poor show' and success was greeted with a simple 'well done'.

I ♥ Panenka

If only the Czech playmaker Antonín Panenka had premiered his pioneering penalty kick on a lesser stage, it might not have been so undeniably cool. But instead, he chose to debut it on one of the biggest stages in world football and at a moment of near-unbearable tension.

It was the final of the 1976 Euros, Czechoslovakia v West Germany. The score was 2-2 after extra time, meaning penalties. The first seven were converted. And then Germany missed. With the score 4–3, Panenka stepped up to take the fifth Czechoslovakian penalty to win the title. And that's when it happened. Under immense pressure, he feigned shooting to the side of the goal, causing West German keeper Sepp Maier to dive to his left. Then Panenka gently chipped the ball into the middle of the net. The bastard.

While there are plenty of modern footballers who still adhere to the old-fashioned approach to penalties, pick a spot and leather it as hard as you can, the long reach of Panenka is felt more today than ever before.

In love with the idea of having their own signature move, players have taken what Panenka did and run with it. Neymar, Pogba, Bruno Fernandes, they're all at it, a generation of footballers determined to make the 'penalty' their own.

And often it comes off. Back in 2018, Rubin Kazan youth player Norik Avdalyan netted a breathtaking backflip penalty during the club's U21 clash against FC Ural. The audacious spot kick was picked up on social media, his innovation displayed across the football world.

But the important thing about Avdalyan's kick was that it went in. During an average Premier League season, not only are penalties not that common (with the notable exception of perennial beneficiaries Liverpool and Manchester United), between about a quarter and a third are missed, which represents a pretty high chance of failure for those stepping up to the challenge. It's bad enough for fans when this happens conventionally, when a player hits a poor pen or a keeper guesses right. But when it happens after a player has attempted their own 'innovation', it feels and looks so much worse.

The poster boy for innovative spot kick gone wrong is the Italian forward, and former West Ham substitute, Simone Zaza. Like Panenka, Zaza chose to debut his innovation at the 2016 Euros, in this instance a penalty shoot-out between Italy and Germany in the quarter-finals. With a bizarre run-up inspired by a cartoon villain tiptoeing across the screen, Zaza finished off the move by ballooning the ball so far over the bar that some believe it has yet to land. Unlike his Czech forbear, nobody has since attempted to do a 'Zaza'.

But despite his cautionary tale, the lust for exceptionalism remains as player after player seeks to have their own signature move. It all makes you wish that Sepp Maier had guessed right.

The Idiot Box

Since TV rolled into town, the history of football in this country has really been a tale of how it and the broadcasters have come together to change the nature of the game.

For a time, the change was slow, TV incrementally chipping away at the foundations of English football. But that glacial pace sped up after 1992; a catalytic moment that would see the arrival of Sky and the birth of the Premier League. Or the 'FA Premier League' as it was called back then, the 'FA' acronym standing both for the Football Association and also the amount of influence that organisation had on the league.

Sky billed their new revolution as a 'Whole New Ball Game' and sold it to the nation via a slick TV advert in which a host of top-flight stars, such as John Salako, Vinny Jones and Tim Sherwood showered together to a backtrack of Simple Minds' 'Alive and Kicking'. The advert also included other staples of English football, including John Wark pumping iron, Paul Stewart driving a sports car and Anders Limpar receiving breakfast in bed.

When the first televised matches arrived, they came with a fanfare, a visual and aural assault of swirling graphics, synth-heavy baselines and a Bontempi brass section. It gave the viewers the distinct feeling that they might be sitting down to watch the NFL. That's until a clip of an aging Peter Reid appeared, parading around the screen like the ghost of the Football League past.

In the end, Sky's 'Whole New Ball Game' proved to be a hit. So much so that the Premier League soon realised it had sold itself short when flogging the rights for a pittance. So, in the years that followed, the amount it cost Sky and later broadcasters to buy the rights rose exponentially to the point where the top flight coins in around £9bn today.

But what worked out great for the Premier League, came at a cost. Pretty much every single part of the modern game that fans have a problem with can be traced back to 1992 and the arrival of Sky. Things like extortionate ticket prices, bloated transfer costs, disenfranchised fans, deteriorating atmosphere, footballing predictability, spiralling wages, Jermaine Jenas ... the list is endless.

And all of this to make fans shell out over a grand for something that they once got for free. If only that initial advert hadn't been so alluring. But we were powerless in the face of its raw sex appeal. Just the briefest sight of Tim Sherwood lathering up his soapy body and Sky had us in the palm of their hands.

Injury Porn

Mmm, how hot is that double leg break. Ooohhhh, I can't get enough of your dislocated shoulder. Aahhh, I love the way your ankle has snapped in a catastrophic fashion.

There used to be a time when the possibility of catching the moment a serious injury took place in football was limited. There just weren't enough cameras available. As strange as it might seem to those raised in the Sky era, fans used to be content watching televised games that only boasted a few perspectives.

This probably had something to do with the wider culture of going to the match, where you stood and watched from a static point. It made the idea of multifaceted angles seem unnecessarily expansive.

With only a handful of cameras at the game, it meant the odds of capturing the injury at the right time and from the right point of view were slim.

But since Sky rolled into town, everything has changed. At the very beginning, the broadcaster reasoned that what mattered most to its army of punters wasn't just the sight of Richard Keys oozing smarm into their living rooms, but also the opportunity to see football from as many camera angles as possible. With a Big Brother-esque sense of commitment, it set about creating just that: a viewing experience in which nearly every facet of the game has become available to those watching at home. Including injuries.

Whereas once you would often just see a collision of legs and then a player crumple to a heap on the ground, with Sky's forensic-like approach, it's now possible to watch the injury unfold in all its detailed horror, a slow-motion car crash for your edification.

And just like actual car crashes, for which a rubber-necking audience has always existed, we gobble up what Sky captures, deriving a sense of pleasure over these in-depth, slow-motion replays that nears the pornographic.

Along with those watching at home, the joys of social media have also ensured that these brief clips of human torment can now be rapidly and easily shared to millions. The football sites, the sports sites, the fan sites, they're all hungry for a slice of this misery, grabbing it, repackaging it and spewing it out through all available channels.

Maybe we would be less keen to watch these moments of human torment if the broadcasters and media companies were compelled to make the clips more akin to actual pornography? If they were forced to include loud moans, a funky bass line, and everything introduced via spurious plot devices, like the delivery of a pizza or the hot gardener taking a break from his toils.

It won't stop terrible injuries from happening, but at the very least it might make our public revelling in them a lot less comfortable.

Inked Up

Once the preserve of whisky-sodden grandads and old prison lags, tattoos are everywhere now. In the football world, they're near ubiquitous, the desire to ink up saturating the game.

The greatest offender is widely considered to be Sergio Ramos, a man whose 42 tattoos make him look like he should be working the waltzers on Hastings pier, not trotting out at the Bernabéu.

Inevitably, because the trend is so widespread, combined with the fact that footballers have too much time on their hands and too many people agreeing to their every whim, a lot of these tattoos are a bit s**t.

Take Christian Vieri, whose right arm's collection of weird symbols makes it look like the tattooist in question had taken a long phone call while working on the job and had inadvertently spent most of the session using the player's skin for some in-depth doodling.

And then there's those, like Borussia Dortmund's Marco Reus, who go in for the 'inspirational' quote as a way of showing their deeper, more 'spiritual' side. Reus's left hand has been inked with the stirring Oprah maxim: 'The biggest adventure you can have is to live your dreams.' But does that bear scrutiny? Would falling to your death from a great height – a common recurring dream of mine – necessarily lead to a happy life?

Other players, perhaps going for the 'academic' angle, opt for a bit of Latin, like Daniel Agger's 'Mors Certa Est Hora Incerta Sua' (Death is certain, its hour is uncertain) and David Beckham's 'Perfectio in Spiritu' (Spiritual Perfection). But if a player is going down this path, it's important to get it right because nobody wants to end up looking like John Carew, whose neck tattoo reads 'Ma Vie, Mes Régles', which translates as 'My Life, My Menstruation' rather than the intended 'My Life, My Rules'.

And lastly there are those footballers who might get the tattoo they wanted but end up with one that doesn't really suit them. Like Theo Walcott, whose Sanskrit tattoo translates as 'Beautiful, Blessed, Strong, Intelligent'. But really, if

Walcott was being honest with both himself and the wider football world, he should probably have had the Sanskrit for 'Disappointing Final Ball' written on his wrist instead.

Perhaps one of the worst aspects of the proliferation of tattoos is the fact that it makes you respect those players who refuse to ink, making them seem humble and self-effacing. Within this tiny constituency sits Cristiano Ronaldo. And surely any trend that makes Ronaldo seem self-effacing and humble can't be good.

Itchy Trigger Fingers

First arrives the chairperson's vote of confidence, like a farmer reassuring a turkey before Christmas that they see it having a long and happy life. From that moment on, the guillotine's blade hangs precariously over the manager's head. It's now a case of when rather than if it will drop. One more poor result should do it. And, sure enough, after a disastrous home defeat a few days later, down it comes, yet another managerial casualty to add to the pile.

The average Premier League manager's lifespan is now 91 games.

The average manager will oversee 33 wins, 25 draws and 33 losses – giving them a 30 per cent win rate.

On average, they won't win a trophy.

Despite his non-conformist aesthetic, former Manchester City and Nottingham Forest boss Stuart Pearce is in fact the arithmetic mean in the top-flight managerial game, ratcheting up 32 wins, 26 draws and a win percentage of 30.77 per cent.

Some reigns in modern football have been brutally short. Les Read, who led Charlton for a short spell in 2006, holds the Premier League record. Despite literally writing the book on football management – *The Official FA Guide to Basic Team Coaching* – Read lost his job after just 40 days.

Although many managerial casualties are undoubtedly deserved, with no signs of even the slightest improvement on the horizon, brutal short-termism has crept into the game in the higher reaches.

How else to explain the bizarre tenure of Frank de Boer at Crystal Palace in 2017?

Tasked with implementing a sexy new brand of football at Selhurst Park in the wake of Sam Allardyce's resignation, De Boer was sacked just four league games into the season. Although the board could point to four defeats and no goals as justification for their action, the job the departing Dutchman had been tasked with was no easy one. Turning around a ship that until recently had been sailing the gravy seas of Captain Allardyce's lifelong journey to discover the lost land of 1950s football, was never going to be a quick fix. But it didn't matter. Palace's form set the nerves jangling and with that De Boer was gone.

They jangled because such a drought of points hinted at a season of struggle ahead, one that might very well end in relegation. And that's the problem with modern football at the top: the swelling fear of the drop. The money that has flowed into the game has created a system in which relegation is now so financially calamitous, that even the faintest whiff of it can cause fearful chairmen to leap into action and jettison a coach they previously had so much faith in.

Whether it's the Pozzo family at Watford, firing managers like ducks at a shooting range, or just an average chairperson getting a cold sweat over the state of the club's future balance sheet, it seems as though the existential fear of relegation now governs our game like never before.

Jamie Carragher

In Debrett's *Guide to Etiquette and Modern Manners*, widely regarded as the go-to book for anyone wanting to navigate the various rules of polite society, it's clearly stated that when confronted with somebody who is taking the piss out of your football team, the correct response is to locate their 14-year-old daughter, fill your mouth with sufficient saliva and then forcibly release it at her. It's a convention that's as old as time itself. Which is probably why Jamie Carragher still has a well-paid job on Sky Sports.

In keeping with the latter years of his playing career, the ex-Liverpool man's defence after the incident was pretty shabby, claiming that he had actually been aiming at the girl's dad. As though, 'Sorry I spat at your daughter, I was aiming at you!' paints a vastly more flattering picture.

Although suspended for a few months, Carragher was soon back on our screens and testing the limits of his apparent unsackability when he followed up 'Spit-Gate' with a decision in the summer of 2020 to defy coronavirus lockdown restrictions and celebrate Liverpool's title win with thousands of other disease-spreading vectors at the city's waterfront. What would have drawn rebuke and the possible sack for most, earned little more than a disinterested shrug from his employers.

Clearly, Carragher has developed something of a 'bulletproof' reputation at Sky. The broadcaster, who first hired him as a pundit back in 2013, is apparently loath to break up the unlikely double act he has formed with Gary Neville. It's a partnership notable for boasting two straight men, a bit like having two Sid Littles. In it, Neville provides the insight and analysis, while Carragher provides the bits where Neville doesn't speak.

Why his contribution to Sky's output is regarded so highly is hard to know. It might be more understandable if Carragher's broadcasting style was an easy watch. But unless Sky's audience is largely made up of those who like their pundits to pepper their speech with unfathomably long pauses and deliver their lines at a rate that comes close to breaking the sound barrier, it's difficult to see why Carragher wasn't sent packing after 'Spit-Gate'.

Whatever the reason, it's interesting to speculate what it would take for Sky to ever sack their Teflon-coated pundit. Maybe a David Icke-esque journey into the wider extremes of conspiracy-theory lunacy? Interspacing his commentary with regular denunciations of the Koran … in rap? Delivering his analysis blacked up? Who knows?

After all, once you've publicly spat at a child and not lost your job, anything is possible.

Jamie Redknapp

If Jamie Redknapp had a pH rating, it would be 7.

You get the impression he's simply included by Sky as a balancing agent, there to dampen down a spicier sauce made up of the likes of Graeme Souness and Roy Keane. Jamie, like a human form of yoghurt, can always be relied on to bring proceedings back to a more palatable average, applying a brand of banality that's almost oppressive in its sheer averageness. 'If a tree falls in a forest and no one is around to hear it, does it make a sound?' One philosophical thought experiment posits. 'If Jamie Redknapp speaks in a studio and everyone hears it, has he made a sound?' might be another.

Every pundit has their own unique selling point. Roy Keane brings brutal honesty, Gary Neville expert analysis, Micah Richards the sense that you don't want to be around when the laughter stops. For Jamie, his USP is the ability to tell you exactly what you already know. He has an almost uncanny knack for describing what has happened in a game at the surface level. There are no hidden depths when Jamie speaks. This is punditry without nuance.

But perhaps aware that he resides firmly on the beige colour spectrum, I like to think that Jamie has rebelled slightly of late. Hidden, here and there, appears to be a deliberate attempt to subvert his role as punditry's very own noble gas.

Take his liberal use of the word 'literally'. 'He literally chopped him in half in that challenge.' 'The ball literally gave him a haircut.' 'He's literally just eaten the fourth official.' Although it's possible that Jamie has simply confused the word 'literally' with 'figuratively', I prefer to think that he's playing with the audience, his obvious errors causing them to view his presence as more than just a televisual provider of white noise, in the process enabling Redknapp to escape from the cage of tedium he has constructed for himself.

The same is true of his more left-field takes on football, such as, '[Everton are] a team of men,' 'Peter Schmeichel will be like a father figure to Kasper Schmeichel,' and 'Real Madrid aren't in the same league as Barcelona.' Such utterances suggest a man who is no longer content to remain footballing tapioca and, through the power of deliberate idiocy, is breaking free.

Recently we got a hint of what the future might hold if he continues down this path, when Jamie, for the first time, ventured beyond football, offering his take on the Black Lives Matter protests and the problem of endemic racism in Britain. The solution, he told the nation, was for more BAME children to become pupils at his son's private school. Tone deaf, crass and offensive, perhaps, but finally a Jamie Redknapp to get viewers sitting up and taking notice.

John Sitton's Managerial Masterclass

For all its in-depth coverage of Pep Guardiola at his whiteboard, moving magnetic counters at a dizzying speed, while addressing the squad in an urgent tone that often ventures into the incomprehensible, it's hard not to come away from Amazon's *All or Nothing: Manchester City* and think it's anything other than one long promotional video for the club.

Despite the appearance of limitless access, it regularly pulls its punches, failing to probe when required and neglectfully turning the camera off at vital moments.

But it's not alone, forming one strand of a new breed of football documentary that, above all else, are resolutely 'on-message'.

They're all a very long way from the nightmarish yet much more compelling documentaries of the past. Think of Peter Reid's swearing masterclass in 1998's *Premier Passions*. Or Graham Taylor's managerial meltdown in 1994's *An Impossible Job*. And then there's the greatest of all, 1995's *Leyton Orient: Club for a Fiver*, a documentary that will always be remembered for the half-time 'team talk' that manager John Sitton gave to his players. A 'chat' that included this wonderful piece of motivational speech:

> So you, you little c**t, when I tell you to do something and you, you fucking big c**t, when I tell you to do something, do it. And if you f**king come back at me, we'll have a f**king right sort out in here. And you can pair up if you like. And you can f**king pick someone else to help you, and you can bring your f**king dinner. Because, by the time I'm finished with you, you'll f**king need it. Do you f**king hear what I'm saying or not?

Each of these, and many more like them, were captivating because the club lacked control of the outcome, meaning viewers got to see a 'warts-and-all' insight, not some carefully choreographed piece of public relations 'content'. In the modern, corporate incarnation of the football documentary, you can guarantee that if Pep Guardiola ever channelled his 'inner Sitton' and challenged Gabriel Jesus to bring his 'f**king dinner', it would inevitably end up on the cutting room floor.

It's a shame because when these 'old-skool' documentaries are still made, the results are always so much more entertaining. Such as Channel 5's *Being Liverpool*, broadcast back in 2012. Although Liverpool were clearly aiming for a bit of promotional content, what they failed to appreciate was how 'David Brentian' their manager at the time, Brendan Rodgers, was. With his motivational speeches, middle-managerial perspective and total lack of self-awareness, Rogers made *Being Liverpool* car crash television, which is something any good football documentary should always hope to be.

Jostling for a Move

Modern footballers are often referred to as 'mercenaries', but not in the cool way like the A-Team. They're not a ragtag band of misfits, travelling from town to town, righting wrongs, just keeping one step ahead of Colonel Decker.

No, in this sense, they're the other kind of mercenary: the actual, real-life, guns-for-hire, men without flags whose only interest is in who is paying the most for their services.

Less Hannibal and Murdoch, more Blackwater. Less fashioning a makeshift tank from the contents of a shed, more the illegal detention and murdering of Iraqi civilians.

In fairness to players, footballers have always had a weird relationship with their clubs. Ostensibly employees, ones that can be bought or sold, they're nevertheless expected to show a degree of loyalty, no matter how badly the fans treat them.

It would be like you or me working in a shop and having to tell the customers about our love for the shop even as they're loudly explaining, sometimes in song, just how much they hate us and how terrible we are at the job we're doing.

Inevitably, that sense of connection is rarely as strong as supporters would like. While there are many examples of players who seem to genuinely love the clubs they've played for, specifically one-club men like Steven Gerrard and Paul Scholes, being a footballer is still, objectively, just a job. And one riven with insecurity. It's unsurprising then that players tend to look out for themselves.

But there are some who take that to extremes, possessing a sense of 'loyalty' that even Michael Gove might consider a little lightweight.

Take Romelu Lukaku, infamous flat-track bully and the man who currently looks as though he's eaten his younger self. When Everton's former record signing joined the club in 2014, he managed to suck all the air out of the fans' excitement by saying, 'Good players have stayed here a year, maybe two or three, and gone on to a big team. Hopefully, it will be the same for me.'

Lukaku then spent the next few years routinely reiterating just how much he saw Everton as a stepping stone in almost every interview he gave. It's a measure of how little he was loved by the Goodison faithful that even as the club struggled following his move to Manchester United in 2017, at one point boasting a forward line that comprised Oumar Niasse and Cenk Tosun, the departed Belgian remained unmourned.

It might be completely unreasonable, but fans expect more of Lukaku and his ilk. Or, failing that, for them to at least pretend. We know deep down that the players we love are essentially dead-eyed mercenaries, moving from job to job, their only motivation naked self-interest. We just don't need reminding of it all the time.

The same way that we don't really want to know exactly what's in those pies they sell on the concourse or just how little the Vietnamese child who manufactured our replica shirt was paid. Sometimes we just need a little lie to get us through the day.

Judge and Jury

'We used to sit and look forward to football in comfort on a Saturday. I think you're becoming too deep. I think you're setting yourself up as judge and jury.'

These words, spoken by Brian Clough in a wonderfully prickly interview with John Motson back in 1979, seem eerily prophetic from the vantage point of today.

Back when Clough made this critique of the punditry world, what analysis existed would have seemed exceptionally short if judged by modern standards. But Clough was zeroing in on the beginnings of a trend that was picking up steam and that charged ahead like a runaway train in the decades that followed.

As with so much of the modern game, Sky can take the blame here. With an inordinate amount of broadcasting hours to fill, and a finite amount of live football available, they fleshed out the role and prominence of the football pundit, to the point where it now frequently feels like they're on camera for longer than the games they're there to comment upon. And where Sky journeyed, others have followed.

No live game or highlights package is now complete without excessive amounts of analysis before, during and after, where the game is dissected in exhausting detail with the relentless dedication of a pub bore.

Faced with hours of content to fill, the net for pundits has been cast wider and wider, inevitably leading to diminishing returns. That's how we've ended up with Chris Sutton (a man visibly pained by the knowledge of how much better than you he thinks he is), Alan Shearer (what happens when white noise takes corporeal form) and Martin Keown (the shadow that moves in the corner of your eye).

If the amount of time given over to analysis was trimmed, there would be no need to ever see Garth Crooks on TV again, bewildering us with his intense riddles. Or sit through another segment in which Danny Murphy gives a poorly thought-out opinion that's less about football and more about ensuring he lodges in the memory of the watching public, vital for the alibi he might later have to give to the police.

If he were still around today, you wonder what Clough would have made of it all. The touchscreen analysis, the forensic picking apart of every mistake, Owen Hargreaves's accent. If he found the light-touch late-1970s unbearable, how would he have coped with the sight of Michael Owen in the pundit's chair? At the very least, unlike much of the punditry world, his reaction would probably have been an enjoyable watch.

A Very Roy Keane Christmas

I woke up on Christmas morning. Deep, crisp snow lay on the ground, the sun was shining and the birds were singing. I opened the window, took in the majesty of it all and then told the birds to rein it in a bit. No need to go over the top. I headed downstairs where the family had already assembled, waiting to open presents. The kids tore into theirs. I was staggered by their lack of organisation. Staggered. After a few minutes, I pulled them up. This is a Roy Keane family I told them. A Roy Keane family!

My wife got me a jumper. She asked me whether I liked it. I said it felt as if she was going through the motions when it came to my gifts. I had expected a little more from her.

Christmas dinner was okay. I liked how the turkey had been cooked and the way the vegetables and potatoes offered support. But, my god, was I disappointed in the gravy. Far too weak and watery. It needed to establish its personality on the plate. If I had been the cook, I would have refused to let it anywhere near the rest of the meal.

After lunch, we went for a walk. What a mess that was! We were meant to move as a unit but the two at the back kept dropping off. I shouted at them, 'We're never going to achieve anything on this walk unless we all put in the effort. It's only two yards! Get close to people, stay tight.'

When we got back, we played a board game. The family chose Pictionary and I partnered with my youngest daughter. I was scratching my head throughout. I was so disappointed by her performance. 'Do the basics,' I told her. We're not even talking about winning Pictionary here, just having some self-respect.

And then we all settled down for a film, *Raiders of the Lost Ark*. What was Indy playing at with his fear of snakes? You can't let your opponent dominate you. Get out there, impose yourself, let them know what you're about.

At the end of the day, I lay there in bed, waiting for sleep to come. I have to say that I was frustrated with how long it took to arrive. Where's the hunger? Where's the desire? Shocking. A real disappointment.

Richard Keys

He was there when the Premier League began, and he'll be there when it all ends. As the last remaining teams fight for the right to claim the only source of water left in England's post-apocalyptic wasteland, a final spectacle played out at the Wembley Thunderdome in front of the remnants of humanity, mutated tribes roughly divided along partisan club lines, Keys will still be broadcasting, telling anyone who will listen that if only the team currently being beaten to death by their opponents had hired David Moyes, all of this would be so different.

Keys is English football's great survivor. With cockroach-like resilience, he has weathered change and controversy to remain in the game, succeeding where others have fallen by the wayside.

He was, for some time, the face of Sky. Where some might have brought charisma and charm to the role of anchor, Keys instead excelled in slippery enthusiasm and commissar-like adherence to Sky's party line. It won him a secure place at the heart of the broadcaster's output, putting him centre stage of English football 'content' for nearly two decades.

Keys had it all – a secure position, an eye-wateringly generous salary, proximity to Andy Gray. To borrow his own vernacular, he was 'smashing it'. Right up until he wasn't.

After being caught making derogatory comments about female assistant referee, Sian Massey, and talking about an ex-girlfriend of Jamie Redknapp's in deeply misogynistich terms, Keys was forced to resign in 2011.

But no worry, because both he and his comrade-in-bantz, Gray, who had lost his job at Sky at the same time for similar reasons, rocked up on TalkSport, whose mission statement, 'Poorly considered opinions for the middle-aged man', seemed a perfect match for the pair.

With their careers repaired, they then decamped to the home of football, Qatar, where Keys and Gray now act as the broadcasting face for the most inappropriate place in history to ever host a World Cup.

Qatar is a country where women continue to be discriminated against in law and stoning remains on the statute book. But despite what is, by his standards, a progressive attitude towards the opposite sex, it seems as though Keys has been willing to make the compromise.

And all to cling on to a game that should have shaken him off years ago.

If in Doubt, Kick Him Out

For all the technical wonders of the modern game, the worldies, the rabonas, the Phil Neville step-overs, there's a dark part of our hearts that still derives a visceral thrill from the sight of a full-blooded tackle.

Although we might like to think of ourselves as footballing sophisticates, interacting with the game at an intellectual level, deep down, when you're watching a cocky winger torment a hapless full-back with an array of tricks and turns, admit it, a small part of you is aching for him to be booted into the advertising hoardings.

In the club game, for sheer brutality, it will forever be hard to top 1967's Battle of Montevideo, where Celtic took on Racing Club in the now defunct Intercontinental Cup. It was a game in which dirty tackles flew in from the first minute as the Argentinian Copa Libertadores champions made almost every touch a foul. Inevitably, Celtic retaliated and the referee eventually lost control. It's always a bad sign in a game when the riot police have to intervene on the pitch and players that have been sent off are kept from returning to the fray by a match official wielding a sword.

Although sudden rushes of blood to the head still occur in modern football, or as they're otherwise known today, Granit Xhakaisms, the era of the commonly witnessed dirty tackle seems to be firmly in the past. A change of culture towards attacking play and greater protection from referees has ensured that while a no-nonsense defender can still boot that cocky winger into the crowd, it will be the last thing he does on the pitch that day.

It has led to the 'Football Hard Man', once a staple of the game, largely dying away. You know the type: surviving on a diet of Woodbines and best bitter, cursed by a lack of technique but blessed by an over-exaggerated sense of aggression, they would prowl the pitches of England, tasked with snuffing out any example of individual brilliance.

Their absence is felt at a primeval level, the lizard part of our brain missing their presence. Because, despite the game moving on from the aggression of football's past, embracing a world of zonal marking, *gegenpressing* and Manchester City double denim casual wear, the appeal of the X-rated tackle still lingers. It's written into our DNA. It's not big and it's not clever but then, this is football, who said it ever had to be big or clever?

Kissing the Badge

The sentiment is clear. I love this club every bit as much as you do. And I'm going to prove it by kissing a small piece of fabric.

But not, as it turns out, by signing the generous contract the club has offered me. Or by refusing to deny those rumours that I'm agitating for a move to a bigger and better club. You know, the kind of stuff that actually matters to supporters. I'll definitely kiss the badge in front of the cameras though; no problem at all doing that.

Strangely, footballers only kiss the badges on their own shirts. You never see players making out with the club crest daubed on the walls of the training ground or getting smoochy with a badge on the manager's tracksuit.

And it's only ever a brief kiss. If they really wanted to show their 'loyalty' then surely something with more emotional punch would be more appropriate. What you want to see is a footballer getting hot and heavy with a badge, a post-watershed tongue-session that reveals an element of lust to add to all that professed 'love'.

It's not clear where all this came from. One school of thought suggests it originated on the terraces and has been copied by players who want to illustrate similar levels of devotion. But surely no self-respecting fan has ever kissed the badge? Most of us show our love for our clubs via more conventional means, such as by berating the players for every tiny mistake they make or sending them death threats via social media.

But whatever its origins, there's a good chance that the days of kissing the badge are numbered. One of the consequences of the pandemic has been an acute awareness of just how unhygienic most human activities are. It's all been enough to turn even the more socially tactile amongst us into a budding Howard Hughes. Will kissing the badge seem quite as appealing when a player looks down at their shirt and rather than a simple fabric crest sees instead a petri dish crawling with the germs of every sweaty player who has touched it?

It might mean that they'll have to show their 'love' in other ways. Now, about that unsigned contract …

Kits

What are we going for? The worst possible combination of certain colours? Whether it's possible to induce nausea just from looking at a piece of fabric? Just how much neon any one human can wear?

When it comes to football kits, there have been some true monstrosities of late. Such as Spurs' 2018 third kit, a combination of various shades of dismal green, which made it look like the kind of damp moss that you might find growing on a shady wall or some other inanimate object, such as Eric Dier.

And then there's Spanish fourth division team Zamora CF, who in 2018 tried to make football fun *and* educational by producing a kit that displayed the body's vascular system. Why? Because what child wouldn't want to wear their club's colours but also, at the same time, find out exactly where all their blood goes?

And how about what's possibly the worst kit to ever be produced, this time by Spain's Lorca FC. In 2013, in honour of their sponsor, Sakata, purveyors of fine frozen vegetables, the club's third kit provided a backdrop of peas. As bad as this was, it could have been worse.

Just a few years earlier Lorca FC had been sponsored by Anusol.

We've come a long way from the days when kits adhered to just two colours (one home, one away) and changed at a glacial pace. Nowadays, rampant commercial demands ensure a much faster rate of turnover than was once the case and enough season-by-season variation to ensure the punters come back for more. There has even been the development of narrative fabric. Today, not only do kits have to look horrible, but they also have to tell a story.

Manchester City are big on this, infusing all their kits with some kind of narrative. Frustratingly, amongst all the marketing horses**t, the club recently passed on what might have been the one opportunity to make narrative fabric great. Back in the 2019/20 season, City's away shirt was apparently directly inspired by former nightclub and the beating heart of 'Madchester', The Haçienda. Disappointingly, all this meant in reality was a shirt that was mostly black. How much better would it have been if they had managed instead to weave a fabric rendition of Shaun Ryder and Bez, gurning for the crowd in a moment of E'd-up magnificence. Surely, a modern kit anyone could get on board with.

Laps of Dishonour

If you're lucky enough to have followed a club that has ever won a division title, then you have likely experienced the well-deserved end-of-season lap of honour. Usually reserved for the final home game of the campaign, it provides those in the ground with an opportunity to revel in the club's success and illustrate to the players just how much their achievement means to the fans.

By contrast, if you've been unfortunate enough to follow a club that finished 13th in the table following a dismal campaign of mediocrity, who then chose to still mark the final home game in the same way, then you've likely experienced the complete joylessness of the end-of-season lap of dishonour.

As an exercise in pointlessness, it has few rivals in the game. Perhaps only hearing the words 'we'll be getting Steve McManaman's perspective on this after the break', can come close to its equalling. They're often billed as an opportunity for the fans to say thank you to the players for the entertainment they've provided.

And who, after shelling out hundreds of pounds to be perpetually underwhelmed and disappointed, wouldn't want to say thank you to the recipients of all that hard-earned money?

And not just to say thank you but also to have the chance to collectively reminisce, to share in the memory of that time in December when the team blew a 2-0 lead to lose the game 3-2? Or how about the League Cup match earlier in the season when a lower league 'minnow' arrived and knocked us out?

And do you recall that great Saturday afternoon back in March when the team didn't muster a single shot on goal? Truly a season for the ages.

While there's clearly very little in these events for the fans, it's not clear how much those doing the lap get out of it either. The whole circus generally involves the players, assorted family members and the coaching staff ambling their way around the pitch, sporadically returning the applause, their faces not quite smiling but also not cast to the ground in rightful shame, a sort of halfway house that seems to say 'sorry for being so sh**e, but thanks for all the cash. We go again next year, eh?'

For all concerned, it might be better if a disappointing season was recognised as such and quietly put to bed, everyone slinking off after the final home game to lick their wounds. Probably best to leave the laps of honour to those who actually win things.

Like I Said ...

Considering that they started from an incredibly low benchmark, it's impressive that modern footballers have managed to make the average interview even duller than was once the case.

At least in the past, amidst the tired clichés and overuse of the word 'obviously', a moment of unguarded revelation might shine through. But no more. The days of shabby amateurishness that once characterised the relationship between clubs and the media, where players would often stumble into interviews ill-prepared, are long gone.

Nowadays, clubs, ever protective of the all-important 'brand', are much savvier. Modern footballers are coached in the art of not saying much, of delivering banality to a professional degree.

Communication experts are constantly on hand to ensure that players remain 'on message', and that 'message' is: 'Be as boring as possible.'

The traditional post-match interview is now so devoid of anything remotely resembling interest that it's a wonder why they continue.

For viewers, the only redeeming element is the chance to play a game called 'Interview Bingo'. In this, you have a set number of key phrases that need to be circled before you can win the game (although, as there's no prize, and you're sitting through an interview with James Milner, the definition of a 'winner' is fairly fluid).

'We're just focused on the next game.' 'At the end of the day ...' 'I don't care who gets the goals, as long as we get the three points.' And no interview would be complete without 'yeahhhhh … no … like I said …', a staple of the genre. It always gives the impression that what's about to be talked about is something the player in question has referenced earlier. But they rarely have. It's often an entirely new observation but one that's being referenced back to a non-existent past.

Surprisingly, all the media training in the world hasn't so far been able to completely coach out of footballers their strange linguistic tics, the patterns of speech and diction that seem unique to them. And the greatest of them all, the tic that only exists in the football world, is the frequent use of the narrative present perfect tense.

'He's beaten his man. He's seen me, he's crossed it. And yeah, I've just hit it and thankfully it's gone in.'

It's a strange form of English that seems to manage the distinctive linguistic trick of speaking in both the present and the past. As though footballers exist in their own, unique, temporal state.

But can it survive, that's the question? You wonder how long it and other remaining quirks will continue.

Already you can imagine media officers at football clubs across the country, sitting around their computers, going over players' interviews, a copy of *Oxford Modern English Grammar* open in front of them, desperately trying to work out just what tense their charges are speaking in.

Surely, it's only a matter of time until they've seen what's wrong, they've gone over there and, yeah, they've just made them stop doing it altogether.

Living My Best Football Life

Look at me! Look at ME! LOOK AT ME! Like a neglected toddler clamouring for the attention of uninterested parents, they're the fans who demand to be seen. Not for them the anonymity of the crowd, the joy of losing yourself amidst the faceless swirling masses. They must be viewed by as many people as possible and all the time living their best football life.

Vizeh at Burnley, Sam Chippek at Spurs, DT at Arsenal – they and their kind have spread across the game as rapid developments in mobile technology and the proliferation of social media have made it all so much easier to capture and broadcast the 'football-themed content experience'. From a few pictures slapped on the 'Gram', to a full day's vlogging, the numbers have grown in recent years.

And like anything broadcast on social media, mundanity has no place. Generated content won't get 'likes' without extremes. Cue a souped-up version of fandom, powered by cartoonish 'passion' and synthetic 'outrage'. No human fan in their right mind could live like this. If it were the reality of following your club, you would be a wreck within weeks.

Although these fans might represent the extreme end of the 'life through a lens' trend, they're far from alone. Pitchside, the sight of supporters enjoying the game via their phones has become so commonplace that scarcely a free kick or corner can now be taken without dozens of amateur filmmakers in the immediate vicinity recording them for posterity.

As is so often the case in modern football, it's the big clubs that seem to be the main offenders, with the crowd at places like Old Trafford awash with cameras, each lens desperately hoping to catch the treasured memory of Phil Jones taking a throw-in.

Weirdly, it's supporters at less successful clubs who have a stronger case of watching the match unfold through a lens. Having one degree of separation between you and reality, the kind that a mobile phone provides, is proven to desensitise the viewer from what's occurring in front of them.

How I wish I had watched Sam Allardyce's Everton through my phone. It might have spared me the horror that can't be unseen. Although, one lens would probably have been insufficient. To truly make it bearable, nothing short of the Hubble telescope would have been enough.

Look What He Did!

Do you remember that kid in school who used to make sure that anyone who broke the rules got punished? The kind of oleaginous little s**t who would sidle up to a teacher and tell them that it was you who had scrawled 'Mr Roberts smells of poo' on the wall outside in chalk, and then smile slyly as you had to spend playtime stood on the naughty wall while all your mates played football without you.

While never a welcome trait, it was perhaps more understandable at primary school. Most small kids are terrible human beings, self-obsessed pocket tyrants with all the empathy of an apex predator. But you would hope that by adulthood, as the slow navigation through the challenging teen years gradually knocks us into something approaching decency, such snide traits would have been ironed out, their social toxicity limiting any evolutionary appeal.

Such hopes flounder in the face of modern football, a medium in which these traits have not just persisted, but blossomed, a desire to see people punished running through so many of the game's less than generous souls.

Crowding the referee to demand action, the highlighting of misdemeanours, the pantomime waving of imaginary cards, all examples of playground s**ttiness that form a regular part of the spectacle that's the modern game.

Like diving and playacting, it's often the 'foreign' players who get the blame, the idea that they're responsible for this most un-British of behaviours. Barely an example of the 'dark arts' can pass before someone like Graeme Souness pops up to blame those of a 'Latin' persuasion. But you need only look at an average Premier League season to realise that you don't have to have been born beyond these shores to act like a sneaky dickhead.

Although referees are technically allowed to punish such behaviour, they rarely bother. And that massively undermines the deterrent factor.

As too does the fact that acting like the one kid in school everybody disliked (even the teacher) sometimes pays off. Take the case of former Liverpool captain and chairman of the Demba Ba fan club, Steven Gerrard.

Back in 2007, Gerrard found himself brought to the ground in the box after being through on goal in that season's Goodison derby. The perpetrator of this offence was Everton's free-scoring right-back and perennial winner of the club's David Moyes lookalike competition, Tony Hibbert. Initially, after awarding the penalty, referee Mark Clattenburg pulled out a yellow card. But then, inexplicably, was convinced by Gerrard to change it to a red.

It was a reminder to the football world that sometimes it does indeed pay to channel your inner child, reacquaint yourself with that playground s**thouse and shout, 'Sir! Sir! Look what he did!'

Losing the Right Way

There was a time when losing a football match meant that you had lost a football match. But in the modern game, the final result is only part of the equation.

Nowadays, it seems almost guaranteed that when a manager from an elite team is beaten by a team that sits ten behind the ball and goes long, the vanquished coach will dismiss the achievements of the victors, resorting to the standard line that 'only one team tried to play football today'.

Jürgen Klopp is the master of this, denigrating any team that dare not roll over and let Liverpool's attacking machine decimate them. Although part fuelled by a toddler-esque inability to tolerate defeat, he also seems to genuinely believe what he says, a myopic perspective that sees victory touched by the hand of 'anti-football' as unworthy.

He's not alone. Other guilty parties include Pep Guardiola, Roberto Martinez and Brendan Rodgers, purists who think that there's a certain way to play football and defeat can only be countenanced if the contest takes place within that medium. Fine to lose to total football. Not fine to lose to a defensive masterclass and big hoof, launched forward to a statuesque number nine.

On a similar vein, but with a slight twist, other managers, such as Arsène Wenger, Mikel Arteta and Louis van Gaal, have on occasion attempted to reframe defeat through the power of statistics. Take this gem from Arteta, who seemed to think he was auditioning for a remake of *Rain Man*:

> Last year against Everton we won the game with 25 per cent chance of winning supported by the stats. You win 3-2. Last weekend, it's a 67 per cent chance of winning and nine per cent of losing, and you lose. Three per cent against Burnley and you lose. Seven per cent against Spurs and you lose.

For these coaches, the focus of post-match analysis can be shifted if an array of alternative statistics are highlighted rather than the one that most people get hung up about, the actual scoreline. They employ a range of tools, possession percentages, expected goals, or in Arteta's case, a stream of consciousness, basically anything that might suggest that losing 3-0 to Burton Albion in the League Cup isn't quite the disaster that most people are claiming it to be.

So, next time you fail at something, why not take a leaf out of their book? Didn't get that job you were after? It doesn't matter if the underlying metrics were good. Your opening handshake was 80 per cent correct, marred only by your leering wink. The egg stain covering 10 per cent of your tie was the only negative in an otherwise perfect sartorial effort. And 100 per cent of your jokes were told correctly. Now if you can just stop making them 96 per cent racist, you might be alright.

Steve McManaman

Looking like a scouse drug lord from an ITV drama who is in the middle of making the transition to become a legitimate businessman, probably in the property game, but who keeps getting drawn back into his criminal past because his younger brother is addicted to heroin and has fallen in with a competitor drug firm.

And, at the same time, dividing his attention between his mistress and his wife, the former a middle-class woman drawn from his legitimate world, the latter a woman he has known all his life, but who is now also having an affair with his best friend, the second-in-command to his drugs empire, Steve McManaman has become a staple of BT's football coverage in recent years.

Meanwhile, on co-commentary duty, McManaman's contribution over the course of a season can be roughly broken down into the following constituent parts:

- An unwavering bias towards Liverpool. Although a lot of former Anfield players occupy the punditry/commentary circuit, few wear their colours as prominently and vocally as 'Macca'. It's a level of partisanship that makes him sound like a presenter from Liverpool TV who has wandered into the wrong studio.
- Tangential conversational asides with 'Fletch' that seem designed to almost wilfully exclude the viewer.
- Regularly growling, 'There's nothing wrong with that,' when a 50-50 ball is fiercely contested. This is then followed by a dramatic octave shift, as a now alto 'Macca' echoes those same words when he sees the slow-motion replay.

Is there a point to any of it? Well, the infinite monkey theorem posits that if you leave an unlimited number of monkeys in a room and give them typewriters and sufficient time, they'll eventually produce the complete works of Shakespeare.

The 'infinite Macca theorem' posits something similar. That if you leave Steve McManaman in a studio, with just a microphone and a continual stream of live football in front of him, he'll eventually say something of note.

It hasn't happened yet. But we live in hope.

The 'Magic' of the FA Cup

Wanderers, the first club to dominate the world of Victorian football, were famous for three things. Firstly, their players, old-boys drawn from the cream of England's public schools, were renowned for frequently arriving at the ground via sedan chair. Secondly, while playing at home, they were the last remaining team to continue using members of the working class as goalposts. And lastly, they were the undisputed kings of the FA Cup, winning the trophy six times in the competition's first decade.

On the first occasion they were victorious, in 1872, Wanderers benefited from an unusual and subsequently dispensed quirk of the competition, gaining immediate entry into the following year's final. It's the kind of administrative idiosyncrasy that you can imagine the current elite of the game asking the FA to resurrect, so keen are they to avoid playing the various early rounds of England's oldest cup competition.

And that's because, for them, the 'magic' of the FA Cup isn't what it once was.

There was a time when the competition was a much bigger deal than it is today. In the not-too-distant past, millions would tune in for the final. And not just for the match itself but also for the build-up; hours of interviews, look-backs at the cup run, cameras at each team's respective hotel. Even the BBC's decision to attach a 'comedian' to each team, there to provide moments of forced 'hilarity' failed to deter viewers.

That still remained the case when Michael Barrymore, allocated to 1984 finalists, Watford, decided to black up and impersonate John Barnes's 'patois-style', a televisual low that made losing the final only the second worst thing to happen to Watford that day.

While much of the pyramid still values the cup as a vital source of income and a chance to have a crack at the 'bigger boys', for many, specifically those who follow elite clubs, the magic of the final and the competition as a whole has diminished. From being something that every club wanted to win, it has gone down the pecking order, with the cream of the game regarding the FA Cup as little more than an irritating distraction from the real business of Europe and the league.

Along the way, the FA has helped dull down the competition's lustre, assisting its decline by pimping out the cup's name to the Emirates airline, shifting the once-sacred Saturday 3pm kick-off and allowing BT and Sky to get their grubby hands on the competition, ensuring that games that were once free-to-air now exist behind a paywall.

And then there was the decision in 2008 to start hosting the semi-finals at the national stadium. Suddenly, you only had to win a quarter-final to get there. And if you made it all the way to the final, you would be there in consecutive months.

And nothing says special day out more than going somewhere frequently.

Would we ever want to turn back the clock, to revert to the age when the FA Cup mattered to everyone? If it meant suffering Barrymore's racially insensitive 'comedy' again, certainly not. But there's something undeniably sad about the trajectory that England's oldest cup competition seems to be on, its 'magic' ebbing away with every season that passes.

Mascots

Do you know what kids love? More than anything they want their picture taken next to a cross-eyed man who looks like he's been involved in an industrial accident. A man just like 'Hammerhead', West Ham United's less-than-cuddly mascot.

These foam monstrosities now form an indelible part of England's footballing landscape, spreading across the game over the past few decades.

Usually there's a connection to the club's nickname, such as 'Gully the Seagull' at Brighton or 'Pete the Eagle' at Crystal Palace. Although each is horrible in its own way, at least they sort of make sense.

But that's not always the case. Take Elvis J Eel at Southend United. As far as it's understood, the only thing that the King of Rock 'n' Roll ever had in common with the Essex seaside town was worrying levels of obesity.

Although clearly created to appeal to younger members of the crowd, clubs don't always get it right. When Everton introduced their first mascot back in the mid-1990s, the results were less than ideal. Dixie, a name that alluded to the club's iconic centre-forward, was a young boy who looked like a kind of homunculus Nicky Tilsley. With a dead-eyed stare that spoke of death and regret, young Dixie never took off and was quietly retired not long after being introduced.

Keeping in mind that most young kids are essentially borderline sociopaths with a healthy appetite for violence, rather than dancing around the ground offering high-fives, it might make greater sense, and certainly be more entertaining for the adults in the crowd, if mascots acted more like Swansea City's 'Cyril the Swan' used to.

Back in 2001, Cyril became a kind of anti-hero after ripping off the head of Millwall's 'Zampa the Lion' and drop-kicking it into the crowd, in the process telling Zampa to not 'f*** with the Swans'. He also went on to throw pork pies on to the pitch during a game against West Ham, accost a rival at the Mascot Grand National and end up in a tussle with Norwich City assistant coach Brian Hamilton, for which he received a two-game touchline ban.

Since marrying 'Cybil the Swan' in 2005, Cyril has mellowed. But while he was in his unhinged pomp, at least there was a mascot that seemed to understand the hate and partisanship that lies at the heart of every football fan. A mascot even the die-hard of traditionalists might be capable of getting on board with.

Mensworld

It's an abomination, they cry. An affront to all that's holy. How dare these women venture an opinion. With an approach to gender equality that makes them sound like a 4Chan forum post, men across the country work themselves up into an apoplexy of rage at the sight of Alex Scott analysing Fulham's leaky defence on *MoTD*.

The abuse that Scott receives on social media is staggering, as a tsunami of unreconstructed men head online to tell the highly decorated former Arsenal and

England player how little she knows about a game she played professionally, at an elite level, for 16 years.

It forms part of a depressing wider trend that has seen a certain kind of man push back as women begin to demand greater equality across the sport. For them, there's a yearning to return to the certainties of the past, a kind of 1930s world, where men were men, women knew their place and children still died of TB.

But it's not just the legions of keyboard-hammering incels who view the arrival of Scott and others on the punditry circuit with distaste. Even former pros have displayed a less-than-progressive attitude, such as when Patrice Evra patronisingly applauded Eni Aluko's analysis of Serbia vs Costa Rica at the 2018 World Cup in Russia.

Quite how Evra escaped the ITV studio with his testicles intact and not volleyed out into the Moscow skyline, stood as testament to Aluko's powers of restraint.

There are those men who, in a desperate attempt to appear 'reasoned', defend themselves by pointing out that men don't commentate on the women's game, so why should women act as pundits on the men's? This ignores both the fact that men *do* commentate on the women's game and also the troubling back story of 'separate but equal'.

The sad truth is that for all the advancements that women's football has made in this country over the past 20 years, discrimination remains an endemic problem in the English game. According to the most recent Women in Football survey, two-thirds of women working in the sport have experienced some form of it.

From the online abuse directed towards female pundits down to those at grassroots being told that they should be 'at home in the kitchen', it seems that, for a residual lump of men, 'Football for All' might be the mantra of the game, but it's one that from their perspective only really applies to those who have a Y chromosome.

Modern Stadiums

'It has an atmosphere so tenuous as to be nearly a vacuum. There's no air to breathe, no breezes to make the flags planted there flutter. No sound can travel, no noise can be heard. It's a dead, vast empty space where life is unable to thrive.'

Question: Is that a description of (a) The Moon or (b) The London Stadium?

Answer: Both

When West Ham decided to flog their ancestral home back in 2016 and move to a brand-new, multi-million-pound stadium a few miles away in Stratford, on paper the relocation made sense. The Boleyn Ground was tired, boxed in and in dire need of investment. By contrast, the London Stadium was new, massive and, most importantly of all, exceptionally cheap.

And so off they went, bulldozing the Boleyn in their wake. But it's a move that has come at a cost. Gone was the old ground's tightly packed ability to intimidate, its snarling proximity, its surrounding infrastructure of pubs and greasy spoons. And in its place came a soulless concrete bowl, encircled by nothing and cursed by seating so far from the pitch that it feels as though punters are sitting in a different postcode.

Inevitably, for the fans, the move has left a bad taste in the mouth. For them, it doesn't matter that you can now shop for pick 'n' mix on the concourse before kick-off. Much to the board's consternation it seems that no amount of dolly mixtures can make up for the loss of the club's soul.

The only solace that West Ham fans can take from the move is the realisation that they're not alone. Across the country, through the various levels of the game, similar tales are told, as much-loved grounds have been torn down and replaced by concrete monstrosities.

But the old stadiums were knackered, the modernists cry. And there's truth in that. Places like Roker Park, The Goldstone and The Vetch *were* tired and crumbling, open to the elements and devoid of comfort. They were grounds that packed fans in like cattle and where the toilets often represented a biohazard, crumbling urinals surrounded by a protective moat of multi-provenanced piss.

But for all their faults, those grounds had something about them. Located in the heart of their communities, they rose magnificently from the surrounding terraced streets and seemed to possess a sense of history that penetrated the very brickwork, humming with the memories of great days past.

Perhaps if their replacements had considered what was being lost, the process of renewal might not have been so painful. But all too often what arrives is an identikit, flat-pack stadium, a cheerless lump of concrete and steel that has more in common with an out-of-town Furniture Village showroom than a traditional football ground.

In keeping with their strip mall aesthetic, these soulless bowls are frequently stuck on the edges of cities, miles from the clubs' spiritual homes, surrounded by the out-of-town shopping experience.

It has created a very different pre-match routine, one that captures the essence of today's game. Gone are the chippies and frightening boozers. Now, instead of filling your body with brown ale and saturated fat before kick-off, you can spend your time instead browsing in PC World or picking up some Rawlplugs at B&Q.

And then, once inside, enjoy the modern football experience: a broad and eclectic menu, seating that's spacious and obstruction free, toilets that don't breach the UN convention on human rights. Where will it all end?

Nations League

In football there are many inconsequential things, elements of the game that nobody really cares about. Think of the routinely inaccurate predictions of Paul Merson or Steve Bruce's trilogy of detective novels, *Striker!, Sweeper!* and *Defender!*

To that list you can also add international friendlies. Few football events stir less emotion than these fixtures. With collective eyes fixed on the club season, only the most patriotic of fans, the kind of people who have faded national flags hanging from their windows and who don't know the lyrics to *Land of Hope and Glory*, have ever cared what happens when England take on Lithuania on a cold November night at Wembley. Aware of this indifference, UEFA created the Nations League back in 2019, a new competition that promised to bring all the thrills of league football to the international arena.

The current set-up boasts 55 UEFA nations divided into four descending groups, A to D, with each tier containing several mini leagues. As relegation and promotion is now introduced, in theory every match now matters!

But wait, that isn't all! Those that finish top of Group A's four leagues then qualify for the Nations League finals. It's a bit like the old European Championships of the 1960s, when only four teams were invited, only with fewer communists (which sounds less fun).

And if all of that isn't exciting enough, there's yet more! Via a labyrinth system of play-offs, four of the places for the Euros are now allocated to the Nations League, giving smaller countries another route for making it to the finals. At the same time, conveniently for UEFA, the set-up also gives giants of the international game, who might have cocked up their qualifying campaign, a second bite at getting in too.

So far, if judging by numbers of those attending matches and those watching at home, the extra element of jeopardy has done little to draw the interest of fans.

Sometimes the introduction of jeopardy works. Imagine, for example, if viewers could send a small electric shock to the body of Martin Keown on every occasion that he radiated a sense of palpable dread. A nation would be hooked.

But the same isn't true when it comes to international football. They can chuck layer upon layer of jeopardy into the mix and still it won't work. Because, beyond the major tournaments, there just aren't enough of us that give a s**t.

Dividing loyalty doesn't come easy to football fans during the season. It's hard to care about a group of footballers who play for teams that you are, in that moment, in the process of actively loathing. It's different when club football is on hiatus and our hate muscles are in repose, but unless UEFA can find a way to change the reality of the season, or just make us nicer people, the Nations League, along with any other innovations in international football, seem doomed to indifference.

Net Spend

One of the strangest developments in modern football has been the tendency for the partisan nature of fandom to widen its scope and embrace the irredeemably dull.

When you see fans online arguing over who has the better kit manufacturer or whose sponsor is bigger, it's clear that our endless search for one-upmanship is now venturing into increasingly tedious waters.

Perhaps the most boring of all is the debate that surrounds 'Net Spend'. To the uninitiated, 'Net Spend' is the headline amount spent on transfers minus the amount brought in from sales. You often see the figures bandied about on social media, an effort by some fans to attain a sense of moral superiority, contrasting their more frugal figures to those clubs who have spent with reckless abandon (and usually won stuff).

But 'Net Spend' sort of misses the point, because it's a far from exact calculation. Transfer fees aren't just lump sums that clubs hand over in exchange for their new multi-million-pound playthings. Publicised figures don't take an array of other factors into account, such as wages, bonuses or agents' fees. The kind of stuff that's just as important in attracting a player to a club.

Even if the figures bandied about weren't misleading, what difference does it make anyway? Does anyone honestly think that when Manchester City won their first league title for a generation in 2012, the largesse that had funded it took any of the shine off the achievement? Did a single fan pause in their celebrations and say, 'I know this is good, but should we not acknowledge the financial advantages we've been given and perhaps dial the enthusiasm down a bit?'

And ultimately, surely getting animated about a balance sheet must rank as one of the strangest ways to express your love of a club? If we really want to argue with rival fans about who supports the better team, at least do it over proper things, such as which club has won more, who is doing better in the league or which team doesn't have Steve Bruce as manager.

Let's face it, if supporting a football team comes down to arguing about net spend, we might as well start following companies, scanning the financial pages to see how Tesco got on at the weekend, to find out if Aldi can avoid relegation this season or to check whether Netto has any chance of getting back into the league.

New FIFA

There are occasions when adding the word 'new' to something makes it more appealing. Think of New

York, New Labour, Papa's Brand-New Bag. All definite improvements on the original. Especially considering that Papa's Old Bag was just a Netto bin liner.

But it doesn't always work. Sometimes 'new' doesn't mean better. Consider, 'new' drug-resistant strains of gonorrhoea? Or the 'New Town' of Basildon.

And the same is true of 'New' FIFA.

Hoping for a tilt at a more positive spin, FIFA's current president, Gianni Infantino, played here by The Hood from *Thunderbirds*, has spent most of his time since claiming the top job in 2016 banging on about how the 'new' FIFA of today represents a clean break from the 'old' FIFA of yesterday. Remember the 'old' FIFA? The one that was marginally less transparent than a CIA black site and riddled with corruption?

Infantino has tried to portray himself as the great reformer, a new broom who has saved FIFA from toxic governance and the grubby tentacles of his predecessor, Sepp Blatter. But just by lifting the curtain slightly, it's possible to see that the spirit of 'old' FIFA is, perhaps, not as dead as Infantino claims.

Take his decision, on ascension, to make sure that the organisation's own supposed guardians of the truth, Miguel Maduro, Hans-Joachim Eckert and Cornel Borbély exited FIFA's judicial bodies. Or how about his recent embroilment in the toxic politics of African football, a mess that he helped aggravate by interfering in the elections of the continent's governing body. And then there's his attempts to set up a new version of the Club World Cup backed by reputation-washing Saudi money.

The problem with FIFA is the divergence between those at the bottom and those at the top. The organisation does great things, almost all of it undertaken by hard-working administrators and coaches, individuals who believe passionately in the power of football as a force for good. You only need to see what FIFA has done in places like Palestine and South Sudan to realise that.

But at the same time, the good work is often undermined by the arrogant, self-serving, kleptocracy that governs at the top. Obsessed with building up personal powerbases and feasting on the spoils football has to offer, they regularly discredit the organisation, tainting everything it does. Their world, one defined by perks and inducements, seems to be an immutable reality, one immune to personnel changes.

Certainly when it comes to Infantino, it doesn't matter how many times you use the word 'new', nothing, it seems, is going to change that.

Neymar

There are lots of reasons why nobody likes Neymar. Those on-pitch theatrics. The adventures in hairstyles. The overpowering sense of self-entitlement.

Then there's the fact that he cries so much. And ugly crying too. Full-on, almost cartoonish tears, like the kind a three-year-old might knock out after you steal their ice cream.

And how about the endless commercial arrangements, such as his signature perfume 'Spirit of the Brave'?

According to its blurb, Neymar's scent 'rewrites the codes of masculinity with playfulness and sophistication'. 'But what does that smell like?' you ask. If it's anything like its creator, then expect top notes of greed and egotistical bulls**t, with an undertone of sweaty desperation.

'Spirit of the Brave' is of course just the tip of the commercial iceberg, one that has seen Neymar become the most branded footballer in history. Importantly, he doesn't attach his name to just anything, ensuring that his partnerships cover many of the Brazilian's burning passions, such as car batteries and Qatari state-backed investment projects.

But, although you *can* look for specific reasons, a lot of the dislike just ties into his Peter Pan persona, the pervading sense of a man-child who has yet to grow up despite being 29. That's right, 29! Neymar is now edging towards the twilight of his career and yet remains burdened by all the character deficiencies and general bellendary more commonly associated with players ten years his junior.

Where other leading talents have matured into serious professionals, Neymar has remained committed to his self-appointed role as the *enfant terrible* of world football, brattishly swaggering around a game that he believes owes him adulation.

It doesn't help that it wasn't supposed to be like this. Neymar was meant to be inspirational, a player so talented that we would lose ourselves in his brilliance. Another Messi to mesmerise us with his God-given gifts. Instead, his career has become blighted with 'what might have beens' and a journey defined forever by the decision to trade the supporter-owned beauty of the Camp Nou for the oil-drenched horror of the Parc des Princes.

And just when it couldn't get any worse, he's only gone and become BFFs with Brazil's new president, Jair Bolsonaro. Because nothing improves your likability more than cosying up to a racist, homophobic, would-be dictator. Although, at least, for the first time in Neymar's life, when you see the pair of them photographed together, he appears to be the lesser of two evils. Which, in the depressing world of PSG's expensive flesh puppet, probably counts as a win.

Non-Celebrations

For all the surface complexity of the modern game, its performance indicators, its myriad formations, its Nigel Pearson gilets, at heart football remains undeniably simple. The point is to win. And to win you have to score goals. Score fewer than the opposition and you lose.

But getting the ball in that net isn't straightforward. Despite the many rule changes introduced to assist attacking football in recent years, the most common scoreline in the English game has stubbornly remained 1-1. The next most common is 1-0. Although players are on the pitch for 90 minutes, scoring is infrequent. And that's because it's not easy. Just ask Saido Berahino.

It's the reason why scoring a goal is met with such wild celebration by the players and crowd alike, everyone recognising just what it has taken to break through the opposition's defences. You might not always approve of how players celebrate but you recognise the emotional response, the need to revel publicly in the moment.

But not every player reacts like this. Non-celebrations, the kind where the player in question scores and then exhibits the same emotional response as somebody who has just learned that a distant yet fondly remembered relative has passed away, have proliferated in recent years.

For these individuals, the motivation is always an apparent sense of loyalty towards an old employer. As recent, former employees of the opposition, so the reasoning goes, it would be wrong to revel in the moment, rubbing salt into the wounds of a crowd who until recently counted them as one of their own.

But while this might make sense if we're talking about a club idol, who has just scored the goal that relegates the old flame, frequently that isn't the case.

What's more common is players displaying a faux sense of solemnity for a former employer with whom their relationship is, at best, paper thin.

Take Nacer Chadli, who back in 2016 refused to celebrate against Spurs when he scored for West Brom. Chadli had featured 88 times for Tottenham in a club career that will hardly echo down the ages. Would Spurs fans have been that arsed if he had peeled away, Marco Tardelli style, revelling in the moment?

And what about the West Brom supporters? What did they make of the fact that their £13m record signing didn't seem to care that he had scored? You can't imagine his low-key 'celebration' going down that well amongst the people who were putting their hands in their pockets to pay Chadli's exorbitant wages. Nobody expects the player in question to go 'full-Adebayor', indulging in a moment of such wanton s**t-housery that you briefly fear for their safety, but at least, you know, maybe crack a smile.

You get the feeling that a lot of this is just for the cameras, a show of apparent humility that plays well in the media. Because I would put good money on the fact that most players are itching to score against their former club. Whether from a sense of disgruntlement about being sold or in response to the taunts of 'Judas' that accompany some departures, their fragile egos will be itching for a blissful moment of 'f**k-you' football. But in the age of carefully constructed player brands, that can never happen.

'Original' Celebrations

Is there any greater feeling in football than the moment when you successfully trademark your signature goal celebration? After all, it's what every football-mad kid dreams about when growing up.

I'm sure that you, like me, can recall those lost afternoons of youth, long summer days down the local park, just you and a few mates idling the hours away pretending to fill in form TR3 from the Intellectual Property Office. And then the anticipation, just waiting for that glorious moment of relief when one of your mates pretended to stamp the application, your trademark finally judged to be successful.

When Jesse Lingard decided to do this back in 2018, trademarking his 'Jlingz' celebration (the one where he hides his head behind his hands, which have been shaped into his two initials, in a way that almost dares you to hit him), it appeared to illustrate just what an important part of the modern game such pre-planned celebrations have become.

For much of football's long history, goal celebrations were simple and relatively sedate. Players were congratulated by team-mates through the 'manly' shaking of hands or a comradely pat on the back. And that wasn't just the case in emotionally repressed England. Even the Brazilians, those masters of free expression, made do with a straightforward jump/fist-pump combo.

Where greater emotion was exhibited, it was spontaneous. When Marco Tardelli scored for Italy in the 1982 World Cup Final, his celebration – fists clenched, tears flowing, the repeated crying of 'gol!' – was clearly not something focus-grouped beforehand. This was the undeniable expression of raw joy in a situation of heightened emotion.

But things began to change in the 1990s, as ostentatious examples of 'premeditated spontaneity' started to punctuate successive World Cups. Think of Roger Milla's gyrating corner flag antics at Italia 90 or Bebeto's cradling of an imaginary baby at USA 94.

Inevitably, this trend bled into the domestic game, boosted by the near-constant glare of TV cameras and the creation of image-aware superstars. 'Trademark celebrations' became more commonplace, eventually filtering down the divisions, infecting every level of the game.

With some players, such celebrations have become so connected to them that it's often the first thing that comes to mind when you mention their name. Try to think of Tim Cahill and not picture him shadow boxing a corner flag. The same is true of Antoine Griezmann's 'Hotline

Bling' and Luis Suarez's 'Three Kisses' (with each kiss of the wrist reportedly representing the three players he has tried to eat).

It's another dispiriting example of the yawning distance that has opened up between those on the pitch and those on the terraces. Because if you and I scored for the teams we follow, you can guarantee that our goal celebrations would make Tardelli's seem restrained by comparison, the overwhelming emotion briefly causing a dissociative mental break. It's safe to say that there wouldn't be a 'Jlingz' in sight.

My Other Team Is …

Like thinking Vanilla Ice's 'Ice Ice Baby' perfectly captured the raw, urban energy of hip hop, or believing that Jean Claude Van Damme was his generation's Olivier, there was a time when admitting to having a 'second' football team made you a social outcast, so beyond the norms of human understanding was adopting such a position.

It alluded to an absence of that attribute so beloved of Brendan Rodgers: character.

While not crossing the unforgivable line represented by the shifting of allegiances entirely, it was still a muddied halfway house that suggested both a lack of commitment to your first love and, worse still, a desire to bask in the reflected glory of a team that could give you what your other club couldn't.

But times have changed. According to a recent survey by 'Copa 90', amongst a new generation of football supporters, the splitting of allegiances is no longer quite so taboo. Their research found that 42 per cent of 16- to 24-year-olds actively choose to support more than one team. Even more depressing, 27 per cent of them support three or more teams.

Within this, many are no longer confined to these shores in their quest for plurality, as 25 per cent of 16- to 19-year-olds now support a team from La Liga (and by 'La Liga', what that really means is Barcelona or Real Madrid).

Somehow, 'glory hunting' in disguise has become acceptable, as a generation of fans have begun to see the enjoyment of top-level success, the lifting of a domestic title or the Champions League, as something they have a right to enjoy, irrespective of where the gods compelled them to place their first footballing love.

Perhaps, inevitably, as football began to treat fans as customers rather than supporters, those who follow the game have started to view their investment, both financial and emotional, from a more commercial perspective, sharing their loyalty around in the hope of getting a better deal for what's being put in.

Weirdly, you don't do this with other passions. You don't get clear-eyed Marxists popping down to the annual Tory conference to see how they're getting on. Or a Sunday morning churchgoer keeping an eye out for Islam's results. And unless you've got a religious get-out clause, you don't get to have more than one spouse, spreading your bets in the hope of landing a winner. And yet, it seems that football, for so long the one passion that could never be switched or diluted, is now headed down the polygamy route.

Outraged by Shorts

Greeted by the horrifying sight of fellow supporters having the affront to reveal their legs within the esteemed halls of one of the club's corporate sections, Manchester United's 'elite' customers cried foul a few years ago.

Working on a similar logic to that of the average nightclub bouncer – that casual attire and trouble go hand in hand (ignoring the fact that a complete psychopath is capable of shopping in Moss Bros) – the club had a strict dress code for its corporate hospitality: no leisurewear, no replica tops and no shorts.

In response to the swathe of complaints that followed the breach of sartorial etiquette, United acted, sending letters to all executive members warning them that they would be turned away from the ground if they failed to attend in appropriate attire. According to the letter, people in 'substandard clothing' ruin matchdays for other 'customers' in the executive lounges, denying them the 'optimum experience'.

Of all the many depressing developments of the modern game, few are as soul destroying as the emergence of what Roy Keane once disdainfully described as the 'prawn sandwich brigade'. Corporate hospitality and corporate fans have become a significant part of the game today, as clubs search for ever-increasing ways to find people willing to fork out ridiculous sums of money to watch people wearing shorts but, importantly, not sit amongst people wearing shorts.

And fork out they do, paying vast amounts to ensure that they enjoy a matchday experience that bears almost no resemblance to the rough-and-ready, working-class origins of the game they've come to watch.

To pluck Chelsea as an example, because what club better encapsulates the alchemical effect money has had on modern football, just £4,000 a season will get you a seat in the Stamford Bridge Champions' Club. For that, amongst other things, you get VIP entrance into the ground, a luxury padded seat in the East Stand and a premium four-course dining experience, the latter providing such 'traditional' football fayre as spiced squash soup, 21-day bone-aged English beef and pineapple carpaccio.

Considering the dress code applied by many clubs – maybe the match itself isn't the main reason why some of these punters are there in the first place. If you're only able to tolerate watching Chelsea with the promise of artichoke velouté (?) at full time, are you really there for the football?

A few years ago, the reputation of corporate fans was dealt a hefty blow when one Liverpool supporter deigned to share on Twitter the contents of the goody bag handed to the club's corporate clientele. Along with the usual detritus, like a complimentary scarf and a matchday programme, damningly, the bag also included a guide to the 'Rules of Football'. It's probably fair to say that if you don't know the rules of the sport you're paying to watch, then maybe that seat should be going to somebody who does.

Outrageous Ticket Prices

Those were the days. The Good Old Days. The days when you could still go to the match with little more than a fiver in your back pocket and not only get in to watch the game, but have enough money left over to put down the deposit on a small house.

But little did we know that the golden age of affordable football was coming to an end. The Premier League was on its way. It represented a new way of doing football, a world of swirling graphics, endless hyperbole and ticket price inflation rates that would give the Weimar Republic a run for its money.

Since the Premier League arrived in 1992, the cost of going to watch a game of top-flight football at some clubs has risen by as much as 1,000 per cent. To put that in context, if the price of day-to-day items had increased in line with Premier League inflation, a loaf of bread would cost £18 today. To which you imagine Richard Masters' response would be 'let them eat cake!'

For a parent to take a couple of kids to watch a top-flight game can now cost more than £100. And that's assuming they somehow get normally priced tickets and haven't had to go through one of the external exchanges, like Stub Hub, places where unwanted tickets are sold to the public for marginally more than the national debt of Ecuador.

But the problem of escalating ticket prices isn't just a Premier League phenomenon. Even further down the pyramid, hyperinflation has become the norm. It can cost a minimum of around £20 to sit in the stands to watch a League Two club. And down in the nether regions at Steps 3 and 4 you still have to part with over a tenner to stand in a dilapidated stadium and watch part-time welders slog it out in the TotalStick Industrial Solvent Premier Division.

But can you blame clubs for charging so much? Despite the escalating prices, we continue to stick our hands in our pockets. We're dream customers, seemingly inured to price changes. And with customers so obliging and so devoid of critical reasoning, what business wouldn't try to get away with murder?

If nothing is going to change and we're just going to shell out ever-increasing amounts of money, then maybe, at the very least, we should make sure we get the most out of our investment.

In the Premier League, the average ticket price is now roughly £32. That works out at around 35p a minute. So maybe don't leave five minutes before the end of the game to beat the traffic (cost: £33 per season). Is nipping to the toilets two minutes before half-time at a cost of £13 per season really worth it? And maybe put the phone away. All that time spent messaging other people, taking selfies and telling your followers what just happened on the pitch is costing a small fortune.

Michael Owen

In real life, Michael Owen must have a spectacular personality. The kind that's so mesmerising and attractive that being with him almost becomes a religious experience. Because how else can we understand his continued presence as a pundit?

Like an underwhelming footballer who keeps getting picked because the manager sees good signs in training, there must be a whole array of people in television who

Paul Scholes channelling the audience's pain as Michael Owen holds court

Simone Zaza's 'innovative' penalty makes its way into orbit

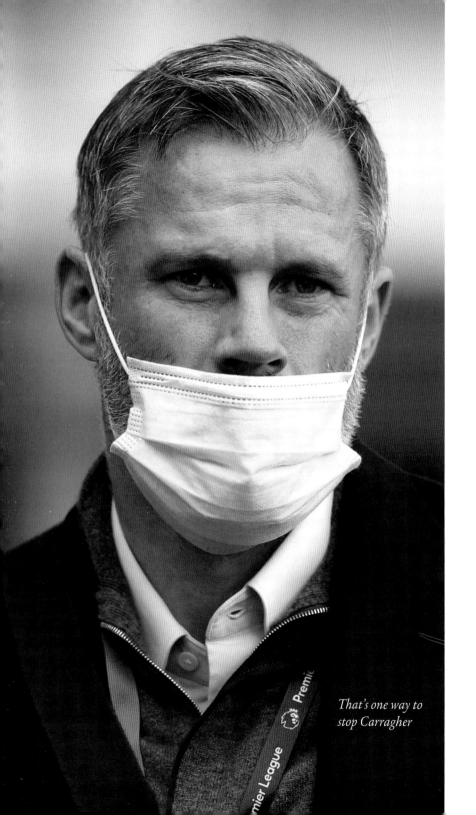

That's one way to stop Carragher

*Mo Salah earns full marks
from the judges*

'I'm getting the letter "L" – Tim Sherwood: Mystic and Seer

'All eyes on me'

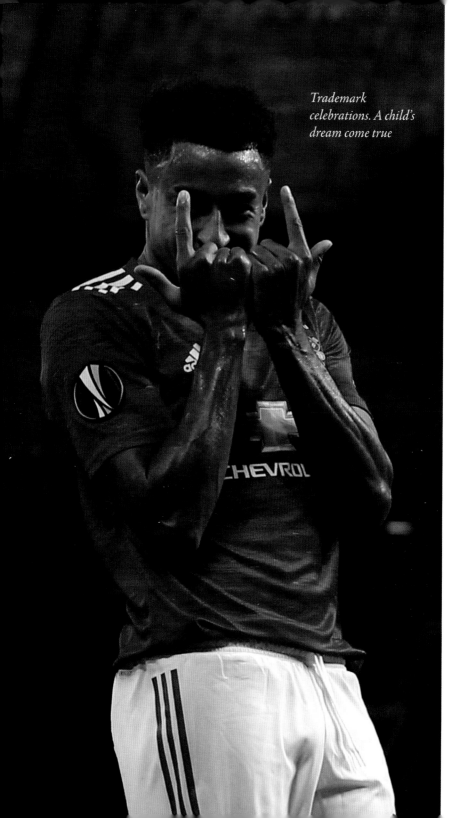

Trademark celebrations. A child's dream come true

The 'New' FIFA

Zlatan applauding himself (probably)

The peace loving, multicultural 'Football Lads' march for 'freedom'

keep putting Owen on screen in the hope that this will be the day when Michael finally reveals to the world the magnetic brilliance of his true personality. But they remain continually disappointed.

However, am I doing him a disservice? Maybe I've got it all wrong and after an exhaustive round of research and focus-grouping, BT has discovered that there's a constituent of the football-watching public who like their pundits to radiate an oppressive sense of tedium. Perhaps for them, the frenetic activity of an average Premier League game is balanced out when the man commentating on it acts like an aural form of Fentanyl.

Whatever the truth, it's worth taking a moment to appreciate some of the things that Michael Owen has been paid actual money to say:

'If there's a bit of rain about, it makes the surface wet.'

'What a feeling it is to be a manager and bring someone on.'

'Footballers these days often have to use their feet.'

'Whichever team scores more goals usually wins.'

'When they don't score, they hardly ever win.'

'It's a good run, but it's a poor run, if you know what I mean?'

'That shot is impossible. I saw Yaya Touré do it once.'

'That's simple as … simple.'

'Alderweireld played really well last year for Tottenham, let's hope he can transfer that form to Spurs this season.'

'To stay in the game, you have to stay in the game.'

'That's only really happened in the last five years. Before that I preferred a milder cheese.'

Parachute Payments

Imagine a plane full of holidaymakers making its way through the air. Now also imagine that three of those passengers, through their own incompetence, manage to fall out of the plane. Luckily for them, somehow, they've got hold of three parachutes, meaning that, while no picnic, the landing will at least not be fatal.

But wait! There's a problem with those parachutes. Due to a massive design flaw, as the wearers are falling, the parachutes, for reasons unknown, begin to scatter a prodigious amount of pig s**t over a massive surface area beneath. So much in fact, that those living below are never fully able to clear it up, forcing them to live with the consequences of the 'faecal gift from above' forever. And that, in essence, is how Premier League parachute payments work.

Introduced, ostensibly, as a way to cushion the impact of relegation, theoretically lowering the risk of a club entering administration due to their high cost base incurred in the top flight, parachute payments have spent the years that followed doing everything they can to wreck the division below.

During the 2019/20 season, six clubs in the Championship received payments amounting to an average of £40m per club. The other 18 clubs got just £4.5m each in the form of a solidarity payment from the Premier League. Inevitably, this distorts the division. Not only did those six begin with a massive financial advantage, but the largesse pushed up transfer and wage costs, making life even harder for the rest.

It has led those outside the protective parachute bubble to spend and borrow in the hope of keeping up, helping to make the Championship English football's very own financial basket-case.

With debt levels of just under £1bn, and a succession of clubs sailing close to the administration wind, the game's second tier stands as the perfect example of how not to run football. Dodgy owners, spiralling costs, unpayable loans, it's as though the Championship has taken its inspiration from a Latin American dictatorship of the 1970s, only with fewer death squads.

But then, that's sort of the point of parachute payments. The Premier League *does* use them to distort the division below. England's elite division has spent years trying to forge a kind of 'Premier League 2', a small mini-division of yo-yo clubs who can bounce back following relegation and relatively hold their own once back in the top tier. And that's only going to happen if you enrich a handful and encourage financial calamity among the rest.

Like everything the Premier League does, naked self-interest is always its guiding principle.

Phil Neville – England Manager

What a day! I got the job! Not on the initial shortlist, or even the longlist, but still their first choice. It just shows you that good things happen to people called Phil.

I'm not sure what it was that convinced them to give me the job. It could have been my spell spent coaching at Manchester United with David Moyes when we powered the club to seventh. Or maybe it was the time Gary and I spent at Valencia. After all, putting together the worst form in the whole of La Liga while we were there is a record that speaks for itself.

Then again, it might have been down to my progressive views on women. Who can forget my tweet 'U women [have] always wanted equality until it comes to paying the bills' or that time in 2011 when I made that joke about spousal abuse? Lulz!

And what about my complete lack of experience in women's football? Surely that has to count for something. It makes absolute sense to go with somebody who has shown no interest in this side of the game and hasn't even coached a single women's match.

Whatever the reason, in true 'Phil Neville' spirit, I'll give it my all. I'll harness the awesome power of WhatsApp to enquire into every aspect of my players' lives. If they have an ice cream, I'll know about it, employing the kind of obsessive, overbearing man-management skills that have long proven to get the best out of everybody. Then I'll take one of the world's most talented groups of female footballers, probably the best this country has ever produced, and I'll slowly constrain them into an FA-sanctioned dogma, stifling free expression and enforcing a tactical inflexibility that's the hallmark of all good teams.

Gradually, bit by bit, I'll wear the players down, squeezing all enjoyment out of football, ensuring that eventually they'll barely be able to win a game, losing to teams that under the guiding hand of a much more competent manager they should be playing off the park.

Throughout the whole thing I'll ensure that I make up for my sheer unsuitability for the role by exuding an air of enthusiasm best likened to an uninvited divorced dad gate-crashing his daughter's 16th birthday party.

And then, just when it looks like things can't get any worse for the girls (I know they're 'women' and not 'girls', but I'll use the term nonetheless), I'll f**k off without notice, landing yet another job that has nothing to do with what I'm capable of and instead is all about who I know. In my wake, another, much more qualified coach will be left to clean up both my mess and the years of wasted development.

And that, good people of England, is the Phil Neville guarantee.

Pitches

Pitches used to be a laugh. Back in the early 1950s, the Wolverhampton Wanderers team of Stan Cullis, one of

English football's more accomplished exponents of route one, were set to face Hungarian champions Honvéd. Wolves' opponents were widely regarded as the greatest club team in the world at the time, their squad featuring six members of the Hungarian national team that had recently dismantled England in a bewildering symphony of pass and move.

At half-time, 2-0 down and struggling to deal with the Hungarians' technical superiority, Cullis hatched a brilliant tactical solution. He sent out his staff during the break to water an already sodden pitch. This included a young apprentice called Ron Atkinson, who later remarked, 'There is no doubt in my mind that, had Cullis not ordered me and my mates to water the pitch, Honvéd would have won by about 10-0.' Instead, through an aerial assault and the nullifying of Honvéd's playmakers via the Molineux quagmire, Wolves turned things around and ran out 3-2 victors.

That couldn't happen today. Hybrid pitches (a blend of grass and plastic), combined with sophisticated drainage, have finally given elite football mastery over the elements. Which is a shame, because the inconsistencies of the pitch used to be part of what made the game entertaining. Players slipping over, the ball getting stuck in the mud, penalty boxes that looked like no-man's land at the Somme.

And perhaps best of all, the joys of a snow-dusted surface, with its requirement of that most treasured of football sights, the orange ball. It was like watching an entirely new sport, as the players did everything they could to stay on their feet while the ball zipped and skipped along the icy surface at a breakneck pace.

And even in the past, when clubs tried to innovate to master the elements, the results were often just as enjoyable. Such as when a handful of clubs in the 1980s, including QPR, Luton Town and Oldham Athletic, decided to rip up their sodden grass pitches and install various forms of artificial turf. The idea was a simple one, the laying of a carpet over two feet of thick concrete. What could possibly go wrong? After all, who doesn't like getting repeated skin burns whenever they go to ground or playing on a surface that allows the ball to bounce to gravity-defying heights?

Football, certainly in the higher reaches, is burdened with a level of predictability that has already sapped much of the joy from the game. How much better would modern football be if the pitch could add a touch more surprise into proceedings? It's that element of uncertainty that the cut-up pitches of the lower tiers provide that make the early rounds of the FA Cup so entertaining. The mud baths that mean the big boys, for once, don't get things going their own way.

Plucky Little ...

You know the kind of club. A footballing lesser light doing everything it can to copy the big boys. Or at least doing everything it can except winning. A sensuous style of attacking football combined with a 'we can probably do without that' approach to defending, these clubs pop up every now and then to the delight of the footballing media. Bournemouth, Norwich City, Fulham – clubs feted by the likes of Sky for their commitment to the lighter side of the game. Sometimes, if they're really lucky, they get endowed with the label 'everyone's second favourite team'. Except that's not really a thing.

Somehow, playing your way into relegation has become something valued in modern football. The good people at Sky will tell you it's because this is how the game should be embraced, a celebration of free expression and attacking verve (and definitely nothing to do with the fact that small clubs haemorrhaging goals makes great 'content').

Why West Brom grinding out a point at Anfield is deemed inferior to a 'throw caution to the wind' Norwich City getting obliterated at the same venue, only really makes sense if you look at the game through the eye of Sky's beloved 'neutral', the armchair army at home yearning for spectacle. For them, the more reckless a minnow the better, entertainment value eclipsing all other considerations.

The same sense of an ulterior motive lurks behind the plaudits such clubs earn from the managers, players and fans of the big teams who, in their post-match comments, inevitably praise the team they've just destroyed for 'playing the right way', patronisingly patting them on the head. How lovely it is, the likes of Klopp and Pep say, that >insert club< came here today with a defence possessing more holes than a Prince Andrew interview. Don't read anything into the fact that we put eight past them. Their principles are the right ones.

For the 'big boys', and our footballing overlords in Sky Towers, one face must haunt their nightmares, creeping into their slumbers unbidden. They wake in a cold sweat, his gravelly laugh still ringing in their ears. Fearful, they close their eyes again in the hope that sleep will come.

But his face lingers, as though seared on to their retinas; the disc beard, the shaven-headed statement of intent, the heft of a man familiar with the pie barm. It's Sean Dyche, harbinger of the 'wrong way to play'.

Be careful, the elite whisper to their young players, eat your vegetables and be good. Because if you don't, Dyche will get you. Manager of nobody's 'second favourite team'.

Poppies

Every November, Stoke City and Republic of Ireland defender James McClean refuses to wear a poppy. And every November, social media goes into a brief meltdown in response.

McClean's reasoning is clear. As someone who grew up in Derry, a place where the British Army killed 13 unarmed Catholic civilians during the Bloody Sunday massacre of 1972, he views the 'poppy' with less enthusiasm than those from communities that haven't been attacked by their own military.

But that isn't enough for some, knee-jerking themselves into an apoplectic fit, which manifests itself as a caps-lock-heavy torrent of social media abuse directed at McClean and anyone who dares defend him.

They decry his refusal to honour those who fought to defend freedom, wilfully ignoring the fact that 'freedom' includes the right to not wear a poppy.

The weird thing about these calls is how recent they are. For much of the last century, a time when the Second World War (the sacrifice that most people refer to when talking about 'freedom') was fresher in minds, football didn't make nearly as much fuss about poppies as it does today.

While a two-minutes silence might have been respected (although not uniformly), the orgy of poppy pageantry that currently marks Remembrance weekend was nowhere to be seen. There were no giant poppy wreaths, no khaki-dressed servicemen holding outlandishly large poppies, no solemn 'Last Post'. And the players were poppy-free on the pitch, every participant effectively being a 'James McClean'.

And nobody seemed to mind. But that halcyon era of tolerance appears to be long gone. As a once voluntary act of remembrance has transformed into both an obligation and test of patriotism, it's become about being seen to show respect. And the more signifiers the better.

Poppies have proliferated in response. You see them everywhere. And not just on people. They can now be spotted on buildings, cars, pets. It's all about the optics, showing you care as much as is possible, even if you're a cat.

And if you don't, then god help you. If that happens, then you deserve everything you get. It doesn't matter that you might indulge in an act of private remembrance, on your own terms, everything must be public. In the spirit of freedom-loving peoples everywhere, put that poppy on now! Fall into line, do as you're told, do not resist.

Qatar 2022

You can't let the 1936 Berlin Olympics have all the fun. For decades, Hitler's carefully constructed attempt to use the international festival of sport to promote his deranged theories of racial supremacy claimed the title as the most controversial sporting event to have ever taken place.

Nearly a century on, it was probably time that another gave Berlin 36 a run for its money. Enter Qatar and the 2022 World Cup.

The story of how a tiny gulf state with almost no sporting infrastructure became the host for the biggest football tournament in the world begins as all great stories do, with allegations of bribery.

According to the *Sunday Times*, Qatar secretly offered $400m to FIFA, done via the Qatari state-run broadcaster Al Jazeera, just 21 days before they were awarded the 2022

World Cup. Throw in a black-ops campaign to smear rivals, and the bid was a shoo-in.

The slogan behind the Qatar 2022 pitch was 'Expect Amazing'. Amazing what, wasn't specified. But perhaps it meant 'amazing' labour rights abuses? Toiling in 50°C heat, their passports taken away, living in squalor and stripped of basic human rights, one estimate suggests that 4,000 migrant workers will have died by the time the first ball is kicked in 2022. As the leader of Norwegian trade unions, Hans-Christian Gabrielsen put it recently: 'If we were to hold a minute of silence for every estimated death of a migrant worker due to the constructions of the Qatar World Cup, the first 44 matches of the tournament would be played in silence.'

Or maybe the 'amazing' referred to an 'amazing' attempt to use football as a way to reputation-wash a country with an appalling human rights record. Along with limited protection for its migrants, who constitute 90 per cent of the country's workforce, Qatar also restricts freedom of expression, discriminates against women and imprisons those who define as LGBTQ.

And then there's the possibility that the 'amazing' in question is the 'amazing' support the Qatari state has given to several terrorist organisations. In recent years it was revealed that Qatar has maintained ties with Hamas and certain Al-Qaeda and Taliban affiliates. It also played a particularly murky role in the Libyan civil war, providing weapons for Ansar al-Sharia, a Salafist Islamist militia group that advocated the implementation of strict Sharia law across Libya.

` In its bid to eclipse the horror of the 1936 Olympics, clearly Qatar 2022 has made great strides. All it needs now is a few jack-booted stormtroopers, some deranged theories of racial supremacy and a lunatic with a muzzie and it might be on to a winner.

QPR Ritual Goblets

In modern football there seems to be no limit on the amount of tat that clubs will slap their logo on in the hope that our pathological sense of loyalty will have us reaching deep into our pockets. Tat such as ...

The Manchester City thong, Everton USB travel adaptors, the Stoke City tape measure, Fulham sticking plasters, Crystal Palace travel neck pillows, Coventry City ice scrapers, the Derby County Sellotape roll, Leicester City 'Guess Who', Newcastle United hand-warming gel, the West Bromwich Albion chef hat, the Aston Villa bread press, Cardiff City chopping boards, Preston North End chlorinated chicken, QPR ritual goblets, the Leeds United missile defence system, Nottingham Forest flux capacitors, Millwall nunchucks, Hull City's elixir of youth, Luton Town Paul Walsh-themed antimacassars, Sheffield Wednesday enriched uranium, Brighton and Hove Albion mithril gilets, Sheffield United's Ark of the Covenant, Charlton Athletic manatees, Liverpool FC virtual Torben Piechnik, Sunderland tripe, Middlesbrough inflatable Jar Jar Binks, Manchester United souvenir hazmat suit, Birmingham City curtain pelmets, Watford 'Make-Your-Own Tahini' kit, Reading medicinal leeches, Huddersfield Town's Anglo-

Saxon Chronicles, Tranmere Rovers vibranium tankards, the Rotherham United inter-dimensional manipulator, Oxford United cultivated smallpox …

Quarterbacks

'From that quarterback role he's playing in, he can add to his team's offensive play. And with his strength and presence, he's always a danger at set plays too.'

Football has always been a sport with its own language, a collection of slang and terminology unique to it. 'Poacher', 'daisy cutter', 'pearler' – it's a collection that seems as old as football itself, so embedded is it in the way that we talk about the game. And almost all of it comes from these shores.

Take the term 'hat-trick', derived from the career of the Victorian centre-forward and amateur magician Ezaxium the Magnificent. A prolific marksman, and one of the few players to consistently perform while wearing a top hat and cape, on those occasions he scored three in a game, Ezaxium would regularly reward the crowd with a 'trick', removing his 'hat' to pull out a dove. Many have since believed that it was the presence of so much bird faeces on his hat and cape that made Ezaxium such a difficult player to mark.

But of late, our domestically inspired footballing vernacular has been invaded from overseas, specifically by our cousins across the pond.

Terms such as 'quarterback' and 'offensive' have burrowed their way into our footballing language.

Of course, a word like 'offensive' has always been part of English football's vocabulary. But until recently it was restricted to its original definition, the presence of something off-putting, like a particularly unpleasant crowd chant or Dennis Wise.

In the modern game, however, this 'Americanism' is now regularly used to describe teams when they're attacking. The 'offensive third', our 'offensive play', we were good in the 'offence', a subtle shift that conjures up images of gridiron football rather than the cut and thrust of our national game.

So too does the emergence of the term 'set play'. Almost since inception, football has got by calling corners and free kicks 'set pieces'. The term, with its public-school hints of coolly calculated premeditation, was fine, understood by all and in no need of changing. And yet, somehow, it's being slowly replaced, eased out of existence by a new generation of coaches more in thrall to our American cousins.

Strangely, considering its reputation for small 'c' conservatism, the FA is one of the main culprits, with its various managers, including the likes of Phil Neville and Gareth Southgate, regularly talking about their team's ability on 'set plays'. As in, their total inability to defend 'set plays'.

It might not sound that bad at the moment, but where will it all end? How long before football boots become 'cleats'? Before draws become 'ties'? Before hitting it 'top bins' becomes hitting it 'top trash cans'? And are we really prepared to live in a world where Phil Neville is changing the way we speak? The answer has to be a resounding no!

'I'm No More Racist than the Next Bloke, But ...'

'All I'm saying is, all lives matter.' 'Shouldn't we be keeping politics out of football?' 'I can't be a racialist, I'm friends with one of them ...'

Football remains one of the few parts of British society where those from ethnically diverse communities can make it to the top. Not management, of course. English football hasn't got that far yet. The game still likes to apply a strict Dulux colour chart to its managerial appointments, very much rooted in the 'off-white' palette.

But on the playing side at least, football stands as a rare example of an industry where a working-class person of colour can get on, enjoying the kind of income usually reserved for the moneyed white elites that are regularly vomited out into society from the ranks of the country's fee-paying schools.

However, not everyone is on board with this. Amazingly, in 2021, there remains a residual, yet vocal part of the football supporting world who still can't get their heads around the fact that professional footballers come in more than one colour.

And it's a minority that's getting more confident. It's almost as though electing a Prime Minister with a reactionary approach to race relations has normalised views that should have died out a long time ago.

Kick It Out recently reported a 42 per cent increase in racist abuse in the professional game during the 2019/20 season (despite hundreds of matches being played behind closed doors or postponed because of the pandemic).

It doesn't help matters that the punishments doled out by football's governing bodies for incidents of racism often seem pretty tame.

Back in 2019, the European Championship qualifier between England and Bulgaria was marred by racist abuse directed at Marcus Rashford and Raheem Sterling by the home fans. In response, UEFA imposed a £65,000 fine on Bulgaria. It was a punishment that Kick It Out claimed was 'disheartening, but not surprising'.

It was also one that wasn't much higher than the £30,000 doled out to Turkish club Beşiktaş by UEFA in 2018 after the club allowed a cat to enter the field of play during their Champions League last-16 encounter with Bayern Munich at Vodafone Park. And it was one that was actually lower than the £80,000 levied against Nicklas Bendtner after he displayed sponsored underwear during Denmark's Euro 2012 fixture against Portugal.

It seems that while acknowledging that racism is a social ill that needs tackling, for UEFA it's only twice as bad as a cat and not nearly as bad as undies; measurements that reveal just how far we have to go in taking this problem seriously within the modern game.

Rallying Cries

Your team has just received a hiding and put in a decidedly anaemic performance. It comes on the back of weeks of similar performances and results. The mood amongst the fans is angry, verging on the rebellious. Almost on cue, the club captain will take to social media, telling the fans that 'it isn't good enough' and that 'it's time the team put in a performance that the shirt demands'. It's a rallying cry, designed to assuage your anger and illustrate that the players feel your pain.

As rallying cries go, it's hardly up there with 'Remember the Alamo' or 'Odin Owns Ye All'. But, you know, it's Grant Hanley speaking, so what do you expect?

Come Saturday afternoon, those words rattling around your head, you wait and watch for a footballing renaissance. At the end of the match, one in which your team has been battered once more and every single player who has apparently felt your pain has just strolled around the pitch without a care in the world, you hope to never hear the words of your captain again, so hollow do they feel.

Which is a shame, because come Monday morning, he'll be out there again. The words will be slightly different, and the sense of urgency possibly ramped up, but it will amount to the same thing.

Seamus Coleman, Everton's long-standing captain, has become so frequent an issuer of rallying cries during the club's recent turbulent history, that his surname has become a verb – to do a 'Coleman'.

Evertonians are now able to predict with some confidence the exact point at which a 'Coleman' will emerge. Normally it will occur after the final game of a three-match losing streak if those losses are accompanied by poor performances and against teams Everton should be expected to beat. Unsurprisingly, there's rarely a correlation between a 'Coleman' appearing and any discernible improvement on the pitch taking place.

The problem with rallying cries is that for them to truly work they need to possess authenticity. When 12th century European crusaders attacked the walls of Jerusalem shouting 'Deus Vult!' (God Wills It!), you get the sense they believed it. The same is true of Japanese kamikaze pilots in the Second World War, who would plummet to their deaths screaming, 'Tennoheika Banzai!' (Long Live the Emperor!) But when it's Jake Livermore telling West Brom fans that the players are going to put in 110 per cent from now on, you just don't get the same feeling.

Rebranding

For years, Assem Allam, the irredeemably unpopular owner of Hull City, has been determined to rebrand his club and change its name to Hull Tigers. Why? Because, in his view, the word 'City' is too common. After all, what club in their right mind would want to be lumped into the same company as Manchester City?

Fortunately for Hull's fans, despite several attempts, Allam has been consistently rebuffed by the FA. For once, the organisation's hostility to change turned out to be a good thing.

But not just for the fans. Probably for Allam too. Because, let's face it, he had chosen the wrong name. If you're going to pick an animal to represent the 'essence' of Hull City, it shouldn't be a tiger. Their slide into League One oblivion in recent years might be better captured by the adoption of a different orange-and-black creature. Hull Puffins for example?

Allam isn't alone in seeking to rebrand football clubs for the 21st century. Plenty of others have had a crack and failed just as miserably. Like Leeds United, who in 2018 decided to design a new badge to celebrate the club's upcoming centenary. The proposed crest featured a torso with a fist placed against the heart, depicting a gesture known as the 'Leeds salute'.

The new badge, which aside from dispensing with the club's iconic white rose, possessed a vaguely *ubermensch* aesthetic, which from a certain angle made it look as though Joseph Goebbels had designed it. It did not go down well with the fans. An avalanche of complaints and a 77,000-strong petition urging the club not to use it eventually meant that the crest was dropped.

It's a shame that if the desire to rebrand really is irrepressible, then instead of turning to the soulless ghouls from the world of marketing, clubs don't instead simply mine their own pasts, looking backwards for inspiration. Because if you go far enough back and have a gander at the club crests and mottos of the Victorian era, you find things that were far more interesting than anything any modern designer could ever come up with.

Take Liverpool's first badge, which boasted not one but two sexy gods, Neptune and Triton, the latter topless and blowing a little bugle. It also contained the Latin phrase 'Deus Nobis Haec Otia Fecit', which according to Google translates as 'Never Let Iago Aspas Take Corners'.

Then, a bit further south, we have Stoke City, whose original crest contains the many things that you would normally associate with Staffordshire's urban paradise, such as a camel, a black eagle and a scythe.

And all the way down in London, back when Arsenal were founded, the club's first badge displayed the heads of three lions with cannons for hats. And just like their scouse counterparts, the Gunners also had a Latin motto, this time 'Clamant Nostra Tela In Regis Querela', which I think means 'David Luiz is Not the Answer to Your Defensive Woes'.

Weird, unrelatable and confusing. That's the kind of rebranding that any fan could get behind.

Rewarding Failure

Back in my teens I had a job delivering the local freesheet to the homes of south Liverpool. For an inveterate lazy-arse, the hundreds of copies presented a problem. Delivery took hours and the reward was meagre. But then I found a simple solution. Don't do it. It turned out that by 'delivering' the papers to the bin, I ended up with all the money but with none of the work.

When I was fired shortly after acting on this epiphany, my former employer chose not to give me a final wage to see me through to my next job. It was a decision that I could fully understand.

But in the Premier League, being s**t at your job, specifically in the managerial world, doesn't come with the same financial consequences. Managers who have massively underperformed, dragging their clubs through months of hell, end up handsomely rewarded for their incompetence.

Take Marco Silva, a man who spent a whirlwind couple of years in the Premier League doing very little while raking in around £15m in salary and pay-offs. Beyond having a lovely coat and excelling in the kind of generic managerial Euro-speak that's beloved of coaches across the Continental game, a linguistic form that talks endlessly about 'situations' and 'good moments', Silva never justified the money he amassed. This was a manager who took Hull down, who left Watford following a death spiral, and who at Everton managed to oversee the creation of an expensively assembled team that seemed destined for relegation. And he's now a multi-millionaire.

In some ways it was fitting that he ended up at Everton, a club that has spent the past few years excelling at rewarding failure. The Toffees have wasted north of £30m paying off a succession of coaches who have underperformed at Goodison. Between them, Marco Silva, Ronald Koeman,

Sam Allardyce and Roberto Martinez created sides that largely veered between mediocrity and disaster. But it didn't matter in the end – when each left the job, their mouths were stuffed with gold.

You and I don't get to do that. Imagine, over the course of the next few months, doing everything you could to undermine the company you worked for, messing up meetings, wasting money, hiring Davy Klaassen to work in accounts. And then, dressed in a luxurious coat, defend your actions by mumbling something about 'good moments'. Now try to picture your boss's face when, after being sacked, you ask for a substantial pay-off for your services ...

You feel as though there should be some comeuppance for managerial failure. That if we can't stop them being rewarded so handsomely then at least the departure should be tainted in some way. Could we confiscate their luxurious coats? Can we forbid them from talking about 'situations'? Might there be a way of converting the pay-off into vouchers for the club shop? Anything if it means that their failure isn't quite the financial bonanza it currently is.

Outside Right

It's a sad fact of life that the older we get, the more right-wing we become. And that's a particularly bad path to be on if you started out right-wing in the first instance. There's not a lot of room for manoeuvre.

So, god knows where Peter Shilton began. The former England and Southampton number one, and founder of the

Jacob Rees Mogg fan club, has journeyed so far along the right-wing path that you have to imagine that his bedtime reading growing up would have been mostly Ayn Rand.

Just on the law of averages, and the huge amount of wealth they quickly acquire, it's safe to assume that plenty of footballers find themselves ticking the Tory box come election time. But because of the game's working-class origins, few of them confirm that quite as publicly as Shilton has.

Although, there *are* some, including the likes of Karl Henry, Frank Lampard and Sol Campbell, sticking their head above the parapet to nail their colours to the Conservative mast.

Campbell, in particular, has been enthusiastic in his support and at one time was mooted as a potential Tory candidate for the London mayoral race. His Conservatism is rooted in a fervent passion for enterprise, self-reliance and, of course, keeping as much of his own money as possible.

Campbell has been keen to adopt the trappings of Conservative life, most notably a love of countryside shooting. Back in 2015, while speaking to the *Shooting Gazette,* he gave the world what's possibly the greatest quote to fuse the worlds of football and Toryism, when he said:

'This year I shot about 30 birds … the banter was just lovely.'

Stood on a rural estate, far from the horrors of metropolitan London, this is how I like to picture Campbell. As bird carcasses fall from the sky, we find him chuckling with his fellow shooters about privatising health care and the country's ever-widening levels of income inequality.

More recently, Matthew Le Tissier, in contrast to the lethargy that characterised his football career, has raced to outdo the likes of Campbell and Shilton. Whether it's questioning the support for the Black Lives Matter movement by his Sky colleagues or clumsily comparing the police's enforcement of mask-wearing protocols during the coronavirus pandemic with those who perpetrated the Holocaust, he seems like a man making up for lost time.

And maybe one day he, and his other fellow travellers, will reach the apex of the right-leaning footballer, the destination staked by one-time Italian import and disastrous Sunderland manager, Paulo Di Canio, who infamously declared himself an admirer of Italian fascist dictator Benito Mussolini in his imaginatively titled 2001 tome, *Paolo Di Canio: The Autobiography*.

It's the kind of clear-eyed right-wing zealotry that you could imagine earning the admiration of Peter Shilton. Right up to the moment he remembers that Di Canio is foreign, and therefore should never have been allowed into this country in the first place.

Slogans

We have Barcelona to blame for this, pioneering the football slogan back in 1968, when soon-to-be club president, Narcís de Carreras originally coined the phrase 'Més que un club' (More than a club).

At least in those times of suppressed democratic rights under Franco, it made sense, depicting how Barça was about more than sport, feeding into notions of Catalan identity. But 50 years on, as slogans have proliferated across the game, they've become less about political rebellion and much more about getting people to hand over £60 for a lurid away kit.

Lots of clubs, but specifically those amongst the 'elite', do it, splashing out on a fancy summer marketing campaign, complete with brand-new slogan and a succession of players posing in new kits and merchandise, usually kissing the badge or silently roaring their approval to the camera.

The weird thing is, it's all so unnecessary. Every season, it's a sure bet that we're going to buy club merchandise. As fans, we seem to possess a near inexhaustible demand for it. We're a customer base devoid of critical reasoning when it comes to our clubs.

Which means we don't really need sophisticated campaigns to get us to dig deep. Manchester United could probably release a range of clothing boasting the image of infamous Mancunian and rumoured Stretford Ender, Harold Shipman, and it would still sell well.

And yet, every season clubs feel the need to concoct a meaningless marketing slogan designed to lure us in. Just a scan of some recent ones include:

Everton's 2014 effort: 'It's in Our DNA'. But exactly what was in that DNA? Decades of disappointment? Underwhelming football? Victor Anichebe?

Then, at the Emirates, we have the Gunners' 2020/21 slogan: 'Ready for Arsenal'. To which the answer for most of the club's perpetually frustrated fans would probably be 'not really'.

But best of all, the apex of the pointless slogan trend is undoubtedly Liverpool's 'This Means More', a statement that always has the feeling of an unfinished sentence. Is it 'This Means More ... penalties than any club should be reasonably awarded?' 'This Means More ... Fabio Borini?' Or is it, probably more accurately, 'This Means More ... meaningless slogans designed to ruthlessly mine the fans' collective identity, all in the hope of shifting more units of the horrible turquoise away kit that we've mistakenly put out?'

Soccer AM

Don't you just love blokes? You know the sort, they like a drink, they're a little bit cheeky, they can't get enough of the bantz. 'Crack a smile love,' they'll cackle, 'we're only having a laugh.' Grab him a beer, slap on some Kasabian and bask in the warm glow of his lolz.

Back in the mid-1990s, very much the high-water mark of the 'blokey' age, Sky sat down to create a football show geared to this demographic, as they posed the question: 'How can we tarnish our reputation further?' The answer was *Soccer AM*, a tongue-in-cheek look at the game, squarely aimed at the kind of man who likes his lager cold, his women pneumatic and his denominators reassuringly low.

The show was initially helmed by Helen Chamberlain and a sentient lads' mag called 'Tim Lovejoy'. The latter became its breakout star, a man whose career has always stood as one of television's great mysteries. Some think his popularity is down to his 'everyman' appeal, a theory rooted in the belief that every man must be a geezer-lite composite of smugness and baseless self-confidence.

While others believe that darker forces are at play and that the entity 'Tim Lovejoy' manifested into existence several years ago, conjured up by a group of aspiring 'new lad' occultists, who inadvertently released the God of Banter from his eternal prison in the seventh realm of Hell.

Whatever the reason, Lovejoy and Chamberlain proved a hit, cementing *Soccer AM*'s place within the Sky firmament. Where it has remained since, a staple of their Saturday morning programming.

Over the years, the presenters have come and gone. Lovejoy was the first to jump ship in 2007, leaving to join the smothering ecru fog of weekend cook 'n' chat shows. Chamberlain hung around longer, eventually being shown the door in 2017, as the programme finally decided to go full 'bloke', a panoramic vision of knowing winks and skinny jeans.

Right now, *Soccer AM* is hosted by the presenting duo of John 'Fenners' Fendley, a man who possesses the air of a Butlin's Redcoat worrying about impending redundancy, and Jimmy Bullard, there enjoying a side gig from his full-time career selling lighters around the pubs of Essex.

It's hard not to watch its modern incarnation and wonder who this show is for? As the old certainties of 'laddism' are washed away by a tsunami of metrosexuality, gender fluid identification and facial cleansing regimes, does a show that until recently still had a 'Soccerette' parading around the studio in their skimpy shorts have a place? With its running time already cut back, you get the feeling that Sky is thinking the same, sharpening its axe at last, priming to finally fall and mercifully bring it all to an end.

Stadium Naming Rights

In a game where little is held sacred anymore, everything priced and everything up for sale, it was inevitable that the long reach of the market's invisible hand would eventually get around to stadium names.

It started over in America back in the 1950s when Sportsman's Park, the home of the St Louis Cardinals, was renamed Busch Stadium after the local brewer, Anheuser-Busch, bought the club in 1953. Since then, flogging your stadium naming rights has spread across sport, the trend gradually making its way to the world of English football too.

Across the pyramid, names have been sold off with abandon, often to the disgust of the fans who see the act as a betrayal of the club's heritage. Sometimes, it has been done more than once, with the likes of Bolton Wanderers, Leicester City and Stoke City becoming serial offenders.

Objectively, the connection supporters feel to the name of their grounds is a strange one. Because it's not like those who first named these stadiums ever gave it much thought. Many just looked at the road they were built on or the area the new ground resided in and thought, 'F**k it, that will probably do.' Goodison Park, Old Trafford, Anfield – these are hardly names that reveal a rigorous brainstorming session. But however lazy the creative process, once established, these names became an indelible part of a club's identity.

Although not, apparently, to Newcastle owner, Mike Ashley, who back in 2011 announced that, as a temporary measure to 'showcase the sponsorship opportunity to interested parties', the club's stadium would officially be renamed Sports Direct Arena. According to Ashley, the iconic St James' Park title was dropped for not being 'commercially attractive'. And yet, somehow, Sports Direct, leading purveyor of Diadora socks and those s**t trainers your dad wears, was considered just fine.

Fortunately for Newcastle fans, who ferociously protested the decision, when payday loan company Wonga became the club's main commercial sponsor and purchased the stadium naming rights in 2012, they subsequently announced that the St James' Park name would be restored as part of the deal. It says a lot about the tenure of Mike Ashley that it was the predatory lending company who emerged from the debacle as the voice of sanity and compromise.

Considering that Ashley was open to naming Newcastle's hallowed ground after a company known for tax avoidance and aggressive debt collection practices, you wonder if there are any moral boundaries that clubs wouldn't cross in search of the almighty dollar. The Internet Research Agency Crucible, The Al-Shabaab Arena, Cambridge Analytica Park. The possibilities are endless.

Steve Claridge's Sexual Magnetism

Back in 2015, the Football League highlights show embarked on a depressing journey into the televisual wilderness. First stop was Channel 5, who attempted to breathe 'excitement' into the format by having a live studio audience, hiring George Riley as a presenter, a kind of Poundland Mark Chapman, and including the breathless stream of consciousness analysis of Clinton Morrison.

When this failed to pull in the punters, the channel switched track and brought in Colin Murray, the younger brother you never liked, to anchor the whole thing himself. Murray, a man who always seems to perform 'knowingly' to an audience that doesn't exist, managed to ensure that the public's indifference to the show continued.

With ratings moribund, the show left Channel 5 in 2018 and made its journey to the home of football, Quest TV. There, inexplicably with Murray still at the helm, it continues today, penned in by landmark TV events, such as *Outback Truckers* and *Disasters at Sea*.

The great shame of this journey is that it robbed the football-watching public of one of the most alluring on-screen partnerships of all time. Burton and Taylor, Bogart and Bacall, Tracy and Hepburn – genuine cinematic chemistry is rare. But when we see it, we're drawn in inexorably, an almost animalistic sense of magnetism that has us in the palm of its hands.

The world of football broadcasting, with its love of banter-literate hosts and pundits, isn't a natural habitat for such couplings, and yet a few years ago it managed to conjure up one that, while it briefly burned, set hearts alight.

The coupling in question was Manish Bhasin and Steve Claridge. When the BBC broadcaster (Bhasin) and the former footballing journeyman-turned-pundit (Claridge) appeared on the screen together it was as though the TV hummed with raw, sexual energy.

It was a chemistry borne of opposites. Bhasin was smooth, slick, professional. Claridge sober, awkward, carrying the air of a man who had just awakened from a medically induced coma.

Their medium was the BBC's *The Football League Show*, a kind of very poor, almost destitute man's *Match of the Day*, shunted at the back end of the Saturday evening TV schedules. The studio would sizzle when the pair analysed the highlights together, a 'will-they-won't-they' crackle of sexual tension radiating out towards the viewer.

And then it was gone. Lost forever, the pair going their separate ways once Channel 5 got in on the act. It's a travesty that in a few short years we've gone from the erotic mesmerism of Bha-Ridge to the winking smarm of Colin Murray.

Whoever sells the EFL's broadcasting rights should hang their head in shame.

Streaming Misery

- Clicking on every stream listed and finding that none of them work.

- Logging on to a stream that's blocked by about 30 non-closable pop-ups, meaning all that you can see is the corner of the pitch.

- Realising that the adverts for camping equipment that you have just spent 20 minutes sitting through are all this channel broadcasts.

- Clicking on to streams that you know don't really exist and that are probably stealing all your data but doing it anyway because the game is ten minutes in and you're getting desperate.

- The evil bastards on social media who direct you to these sites.

- Continually refreshing a problematic stream and then realising that you've just watched the same throw-in eight times.

- Due to the inevitable time lag, living your football life about three minutes behind everyone else.

- Pop-up windows offering Russian brides, Asian pornography and penis extensions.

- Those same pop-ups reappearing on your computer days later, when you least expect them, although usually just as the kids are walking past.

- Having the stream shut down and then logging on a few minutes later to see that you've missed a goal.

- Trying to follow Arabic commentary and only being able to pick out the word 'Sigurdsson'.

- Realising that Andy Townsend is still getting work.

ekkers

According to the history books, the first nutmeg to occur in English football took place in a match between Old Etonians and Old Harrovians at The Oval, in London on 25 September 1881. The player responsible for this bit of innovation was the notorious Victorian dandy, Sir Arthur Heathcote-Nutmeg.

For some time, Sir Arthur's innovative nature had been pushing both the boundaries of the game and the patience of the FA.

He had already caused outrage a few months earlier when he had chosen to celebrate scoring the winner against Old Westminsters by hugging the team-mate nearest to him, an act that was considered borderline 'sexual deviancy' by the FA. He also to this date remains the only footballer to have ever played an entire match while accompanied by his valet.

On that fateful afternoon, his ostentatious 'nutmeg', as it became known, was a step too far. Sir Arthur was banned from the game for life by the FA, who hoped that so severe a punishment would act as a deterrent to others considering such 'wanton displays of naked individualism'.

And for more than 100 years, the tide was mostly held back. English football remained a game defined by a rarity of individual flair. While other countries wowed the world with tricks, turns and nutmegs, the English stuck doggedly to grunt and grind.

But no more. Today, the lust for the more 'flamboyant' side of football in England is endemic. It bleeds through the game, from the heights of the Premier League right down to kids starting their football journey. It's even acquired its own nomenclature, 'Tekkers', a catch-all term to cover anything that traditionalists would once dismiss as 'fancy foreign bollocks'.

On YouTube and social media, the love of Tekkers is truly revealed, countless videos and clips of Cruyff turns, elasticos, Maradonas, rainbow flicks, no-look shots, swaz-shots, the list goes on. There are even those who specialise in Tekkers content, such as the F2 Freestylers.

For the F2, and others like them, there's a certain etiquette surrounding Tekkers. First, the 'Tekkee' should react to their successful 'Tekker' as though it's the most natural thing in the world, exhibiting a near-slappable sense of insouciance. By contrast, those watching must respond as though what has occurred has confounded their understanding of the known universe. This is particularly the case for 'outrageous Tekkers', a sub-strata of the genre, which requires those watching to temporarily lose their minds.

The depressing thing about the elevation of Tekkers, both online and on the pitch, has been the near deification of the one player that everyone hated growing up, the 'showboater'. That one kid in your team who would spend the whole game hogging the ball and trying to beat the entire opposition on his own through his arsenal of only intermittently successful skills and tricks. The kind of knobhead who never bothered tracking back and who lost the ball way more than he won it.

Even the FA are on board, encouraging young footballers to follow the path of the showboater and embrace Tekkers as much as possible. They've come a long way from the days of Heathcote-Nutmeg. Although, it's still frowned upon to take your valet on to the pitch.

Tim Sherwood

Since retiring from the professional game in 2005, Tim Sherwood has spent the following years searching for his place in the world.

For a time, coaching seemed to be the answer. At Spurs, Aston Villa and finally Swindon Town he found chairmen willing to take a punt on his singular 'no guts, no glory … but increasingly no victories' approach to football management. Mediocre at White Hart Lane, disastrous at the other two, sadly for Timothy his managerial career soon ran out of steam.

Perhaps aware of his inadequacies, Sherwood had attempted throughout his time as a coach to dazzle and deflect with an array of sleight of hand. First was his pioneering adoption of the 'sports gilet'. Forget the results and atrocious football, this sartorial innovation seemed to suggest 'concentrate on the fact that my coat doesn't have any arms'.

When that didn't work, next came his self-appointed role as English football's 'straight-talker', a man who would 'shoot from the hip'. Whether publicly bad-mouthing his players, bluntly taking pundits to task for criticising his team's poor performances or stating with conviction his dislike of foreign cheeses, this was a man who would say what he meant.

Although neither approach saved him from the chop, at least the latter allowed him to segue seamlessly into the world of punditry, where straight talking and a hostility to Brie always finds a receptive audience.

There seems to be a statutory remit at Sky for a proportion of its broadcasting time to be given over to middle-aged white men to ramble uninformatively and unimaginatively about the game. So, there Sherwood sits, fulfilling this role, comparing Steve Bruce to Marcelo Bielsa, or telling the audience at home that struggling West Brom might get relegated.

But perhaps unsettled by the precarious and short-lived nature of his managerial stints, the former Blackburn Rovers captain looks to have already laid the foundations for another career just in case his punditry gig ever dries up. It's one in which the world will get to meet his next incarnation: Tim Sherwood, Mystic and Seer.

We first got a taste of his skills when, just before Roberto Firmino headed in from a corner in the dying moments of Liverpool's game against Spurs at Anfield in December 2020, Sherwood proclaimed:

'Another corner. I'm not too worried about this corner … I think Tottenham have got the dominance in the air.'

Moving beyond the world of football, a recently discovered document revealed a list of other predictions Sherwood was working on during 2020, including:

'There's no chance at all that the US president will advise his country's citizens to ingest Dettol.'

'People say that stockpiling ammonium nitrate in the port of Beirut is dangerous, but I can't see it being a problem.'

'Another mutation of COVID-19? I'm not too worried. Boris Johnson seems to have dominance over the virus.'

Time Wasting

According to Einstein's general theory of relativity, if anyone wanted to watch time stretch and decelerate, they would have to make a 1,000-light-year journey to our nearest black hole in the Telescopium constellation. There, because of a phenomenon known as gravitational time dilation, they could watch time run at a slower rate as they edged closer to the black hole's centre, the singularity.

Although, before they actually reached that final point, the gravitational mass of the black hole would have smashed their bodies to pieces at an atomic level, a process believed to be only marginally more painful than sitting through Olly Murs's 2011 DVD, *The 7 Deadly Sins of Football*.

Of course, Einstein was writing about this stuff back in the early 1900s, a time when football was still in its relative infancy. So, it's forgivable that he made no reference to another, much more accessible part of the universe where time behaves equally strangely – namely, goal kicks at the end of matches.

Under the right conditions, typically the side of the goalkeeper in question holding on to a narrow, threatened lead, it's possible for time to stretch and slow down almost to the point of infinity. When occurring, a minute can feel like an eternity as the man in green strolls to retrieve the ball, drops it, picks it up again slowly, looks at it for a few seconds, places it down, fiddles with it for a bit, steps backward, picks up a towel to wipe his hands, throws the towel back into the goal, kicks the post with his studs, takes a few steps forward, feints a short pass, then takes a few steps back again, kicks the post once more, runs forward and eventually leathers the ball out of play.

It's a routine that forms part of a wider pantomime that gets umbrellaed as 'time wasting' or 'running down the clock'. And for those whose teams are on the receiving end of it, it can be one of the most infuriating aspects of football.

Along with the time-bending goal kick, other contributors to the phenomenon include the sudden appeal of corner flags, injury-time substitutions and Oscar-winning injuries.

The last of these can sometimes make the blood pressure of opposition supporters verge into the stroke territory. There are few sights less edifying in football than watching a player fall to the ground under the flimsiest of touches to kill precious minutes as the physio makes their way on to the pitch to treat this terrible injury (which seconds later will have miraculously healed).

And they *are* 'precious' minutes. Everyone in that stadium has paid handsomely to enjoy them. Such is the cost of modern football, that if you're watching a Premier League team run down the clock for six minutes, then at the very minimum that's cost you about £2.

Just rooting around my local charity shop today, for that wasted money I could have bought one of the following: a second-hand copy of *Star Trek II: The Wrath of Khan* (with director's commentary), a 1,000-piece jigsaw depicting some lovely shire ponies or a dog-eared copy of William Roache's autobiography *Soul on the Street*. That's a significant opportunity cost I'm enduring for those wasted minutes. Pack it in!

Transfer Gossip

There are lots of other things to hate Rupert Murdoch for, such as the poisoning of political discourse in the UK, the return of nativism across the Western world and the bankrolling of *Speed 2: Cruise Control*. They're just a handful of his crimes against humanity, a wide and extensive list to which you can also add the creation of arguably the most pointless but ubiquitous aspect of modern football: Transfer Gossip.

The year was 1969. As Don Revie's Leeds reigned as English champions and the country's love affair with Angel Delight was only just beginning in earnest, Rupert Murdoch was taking the first steps on the path that would ultimately lead to the creation of his evil empire. Think of him as a bit like Senator Palpatine in *The Phantom Menace,* only with less charm but considerably more malevolence.

He had recently acquired a left-leaning, Labour-supporting British newspaper called *The Sun* and was in the process of shifting it rightwards and turning it into a tabloid. But the Australian Sith Lord got a bit of bad news with his tabloid plan. A limited number of suitable printing presses meant the first editions of each paper would have to be finished en route to newsagents long before the final whistle of evening football matches had blown.

This was a problem for a title that had football fans in mind as its key audience. So, Murdoch got creative, conjuring up a solution that not only overcame the hurdle to produce what would soon become Britain's most popular paper, but also inadvertently created something that would prove to be so much worse than *The Sun.*

The solution was to fill the first edition with transfer gossip stories (on pages that would be replaced by match reports later). The idea turned out to be a hit. So much so that when Murdoch got another printing press not long after, meaning *The Sun* had no need for transfer gossip, its subsequent dropping caused outrage amongst the paper's punters, who demanded its reinstatement.

Since then, with each passing season, transfer gossip has taken up more and more column inches. At the current rate of expansion, it's envisaged that by the year 2050 all football reporting will be transfer-based, an endless cycle of rumour, speculation and the occasional actual signing.

In many ways, transfer gossip is the essence of Murdoch. Frequently baseless reporting and a form of literary content that somehow leaves you feeling worse for engaging with it. All it's really lacking is racism and tits.

And yet, it's so hard to resist. In the vast and expansive world of football writing, transfer gossip is the fat-filled, sugar-packed snack. Easy, accessible and tasty. We know it's not doing us any good, but it's so tantalising that it's hard to say no.

Twitter

The Greeks knew it as Pandora's Box, vessel of the world's evil. The Aztecs called it Mictlantecuhtli – bringer of darkness. In Aksumite culture, its name was Zat-Badar, devourer of worlds.

Today, we know it simply as 'Twitter'.

Jack Dorsey's brainchild has found a receptive home amongst the angry and bitter, of which we football supporters comprise around 80 per cent of our nation's stock.

Whereas fans were once separated by geography and any violent interactions with opposition supporters had to take place physically, social media has changed all that. Now, you can have a pop at other fans from anywhere in the world and you can do so from the safety of your own home.

It's created a condition on Twitter that psychologists refer to as 'Emboldened S**thouse Syndrome' or ESS for short. Those afflicted with ESS suffer from a pathological need to pick virtual fights with opposition fans, while at the same time suffering from a complete absence of self-awareness and skin so paper thin that even the mildest of insults can cut right through it.

Although many sufferers act alone, sometimes a collective mass of ESS can coalesce online, usually in response to some perceived insult to their club of choice. The wounded gather together to create what's known as a 'Bellend Tsunami' – a rolling mass of perspective-free hate focused against the perpetrator of the 'insult'. The aim is for those targeted to be effectively drowned under the sheer weight of GIFS, emojis and private messages telling them that they should die.

Players don't escape its reach either. Back in September 2020, the young Liverpool full-back, Nico Williams received a torrent of abuse from Liverpool fans after being at fault for one of the goals in his team's 7-2 demolition of Lincoln City in the League Cup.

In response to the deluge, which let's remember took place in the aftermath of a comprehensive victory, Williams had to black out his Twitter account, a notable example of someone connected to the club purposefully making the decision to walk alone.

Sometimes clubs get in on the act too, such as when Leeds United went to town on Karen Carney after she claimed that the first COVID-19 lockdown, and the following break in football, played a part in the club's promotion to the Premier League. In response, Leeds, who disagreed, set the social media hounds upon her. The inevitable deluge of misogynistic bile that flowed eventually forced the former

Chelsea winger to delete her Twitter account.

In Aksumite culture it was believed that Zat-Badar would only be defeated when the great god Medr came down to earth on his two-headed golden dragon, smiting the great evil with his sword of fire. So, fingers crossed ...

Gordon Strachan's Unified Theory of Selective Breeding

While Jose Mourinho might be the undisputed king of excuses, a man who regularly blames anything and anyone but himself for disappointing performances, he's far from alone in the modern game, as players and managers desperately search for reasons to avoid admitting their own shortcomings.

Take Gordon Strachan, the man in charge of Scotland's ultimately doomed attempt to qualify for the 2018 World Cup. At the end of his tenure, rather than acknowledge his own mistakes, which included a certain tactical inflexibility and a propensity to consider English-based footballers over those playing in Scotland, Strachan instead opted to tap into his inner eugenicist and claim the national team's failure was due to the fact that the Scottish were genetically smaller than other nations. In a move straight out of the Josef Mengele playbook, his long-term solution to this problem was to selectively breed bigger Scottish men and women together.

But it's not just managers who grasp at any excuse to avoid acknowledging their errors. Back in 2019, Crystal Palace goalkeeper Wayne Hennessey was photographed doing what, to the entire world, looked like a Nazi salute, complete with hand over lip 'Hitler-stylee' pose. But the mistake was all ours, claimed Hennessey, who stated that: 'I waved and shouted at the person taking the picture to get on with it and at the same time put my hand over my mouth to make the sound carry.' He added that any resemblance to the Nazi gesture was 'absolutely coincidental'.

And who amongst us hasn't done exactly that? Because, instinctively, when we want someone to do something quicker, our natural recourse is the Nazi salute.

But just in case common sense did not prevail, Hennessey had another defence up his sleeve, putting faith in the old 'complete ignorance' gambit. Because, apparently, Wayne couldn't have been doing what people thought he was doing because not only had he never heard of the 'Nazi salute', but he also didn't even know who Hitler was. You know, Hitler, the most famous individual of the 20th century.

Amazingly, it was a defence that the FA chose to accept.

Perhaps inspired by the unseemly wriggling of those who play and manage in the game, supporters have got into the act of late. Back in 2019, after Liverpool had been defeated by title rivals Manchester City at the Etihad, *The*

Anfield Wrap claimed that the Reds had been foiled by deliberately long grass, with one of the presenters saying:

> I could not believe the length of the Manchester City pitch ... The amount to which it cut up, the fact that it didn't look well – it looked like a pitch that had been prepared for one thing. To stop fast passing.

From beneath the comfort of their tinfoil hats, the image of Pep Guardiola, out on the pitch, fertilizer in one hand, ruler in the other, made perfect sense. Just another example of the game's inability to accept mundane reality, the fact that your team simply wasn't good enough, that Hitler salutes are an unacceptable way to attract attention and that blaming the apparent genetic shortcomings of an entire nation is no excuse for failing to select Leigh Griffiths.

Unnecessarily Inconvenient Kick-Off Times

Richard Masters: Adventures in Time and Space, was always going to be a tough sell. Where Dr Who might battle Daleks, Zygons and various other strange alien races, the Premier League's plan for a big budget TV series starring their titular chief executive simply had him going backwards and forwards through the ages to provide consistent and effective administrative oversight to a number of beleaguered sporting organisations.

Even the inclusion of Greg Clarke as Masters's sexy sidekick wasn't enough for the idea to be picked up by any broadcaster. But although the pitch failed, at least it represented a tacit admission that England's elite division possessed something that it had long been rumoured to own, namely the capacity to travel through time and space.

How else can we explain the increasingly bizarre kick-off times that are rolled out every season? Of course, the people who run the league think nothing of expecting Newcastle fans to make a 12:30 kick-off in Brighton, when for them making such a trip would take mere seconds via the comfort and ease of their own TARDIS.

Following your club away from home is a labour of love. It's expensive, time-consuming and, if you lose, soul crushing. And considering that in the Premier League losing is common, with away teams only winning around a quarter of the time, it seems clear that the travelling army of supporters often represents football at its most dedicated, ignoring the likelihood of an away defeat simply to be there in solidarity.

Which makes s**tting on them such a 'Premier League' thing to do. Of course, a league that has spent nearly three decades exploiting supporters would think nothing of making their lives so much harder.

And the punishments doled out to this travelling army seem to get worse year by year as the Premier League and its broadcasters have gradually widened the hours in which games can take place: Friday night, Saturday lunchtime, Sunday afternoon, Monday evening. What constitutes the 'weekend' has expanded to the point of implausibility under the League's guiding hand, so much so that if Richard

Masters ever invites you out for a 'weekend' bender, be very wary.

The frustrating thing about all this is the fact that rather than just scuttling around the country to watch matches, the Premier League could be using their technology for the good of the game, going back in time to correct some of the great wrongs of football history, such as Maradona's hand of god, Lampard's phantom goal or David Beckham's cornrow braids. It's all such a waste.

Unscrupulous Owners

Hum to yourself a *Top of the Pops*-style theme tune as the voice of cheesily cheerful commercial radio DJ says: 'And here we go, the countdown of English football's worst owners, from ten all the way to one!'

10
Francesco Becchetti
Leyton Orient 2014–2017

In just two and a half seasons as owner, the Italian waste-management magnate turned Leyton Orient into a non-league club and almost drove them to the point of destruction. It was a reign that also featured an unsuccessful reality TV show, multiple managers, persistent reports of meddling in team affairs, a scattergun player-recruitment policy, financial freefall and a six-match ban for kicking assistant manager Andy Hessenthaler.

By the time Becchetti finally sold up in 2017, Orient were playing in the National League, having been relegated out of the Football League for the first time in their history.

9
The Oyston Family
Blackpool 1988–2019

It takes a special kind of crapness to make mismanagement a family affair, but that's exactly what the Oystons did at Blackpool.

Years of drift, financial chicanery and hostility towards the fans came to a head when father and son duo, Owen and Karl were found guilty of the 'illegitimate stripping' of Blackpool's assets, paying £26m out to companies they owned.

They ended up having to pay it all back, the huge sum forcing them to finally sell up in 2019, much to the fans' delight.

8
Ken Richardson
Doncaster Rovers 1993–1998

Richardson arrived as Doncaster's 'saviour' in the early 1990s, taking control with one aim in mind – the building of a new stadium (which would, coincidentally, also allow him to cream off the profits from the sale of the old ground's lucrative land).

But that plan was scuppered after the local council blocked the move. In response, a furious Richardson hatched a plan. Two local scallies were hired to burn down Belle Vue with an aim to force the council's hand. The only glitch? The arsonists were idiots. One of them dropped his mobile at the scene. South Yorkshire Police eventually linked the crime back to the club's owner, who was later sentenced to four years behind bars.

Between the arson attack and his conviction, Richardson also oversaw Doncaster's relegation to the National League.

7
Peter Ridsdale
Leeds United 1997–2003

When your disastrous time in charge of a club gives rise to its own verb, you know you're doing something special. Ridsdale's overspending crippled the Yorkshire club, a debt-fuelled spiral that saw them slide out of the Premier League, through the Championship and into League One. And with that, to do 'a Leeds' entered the footballing vernacular.

When Ridsdale called it a day in March 2003, the club was valued at £12m with debts of six times that. 'It is a myth that we overspent,' Ridsdale later claimed. The 70 company cars, regular private jet hire and the owner's £20 a month goldfish habit would suggest otherwise.

6
Tom Hicks and George Gillett Jr
Liverpool 2007–2010

Bringing one of the giants of world football to its knees is no mean feat. But that's exactly what Tom Hicks and George Gillett Jr managed during a three-year reign of terror at Anfield.

Having bought Liverpool with loans, they eventually saddled the club with so much debt that interest payments amounted to around £35m per year. That's one 'Andy Carroll' in old money.

By the end of their tenure, the working relationship between Hicks and Gillett had broken down, the club was on the precipice of going into administration and Joe Cole was their marquee summer signing.

After being sent packing by a high court judge, they eventually walked away empty-handed.

5
Venky's
Blackburn Rovers 2010–ongoing

Once you've conquered the world of poultry, what else is there? It turns out the answer to that question is: Blackburn Rovers.

Back in 2010, the club was taken over by the Venky family, India's premier chicken magnates.

And in the same way that chicken processing takes a healthy living creature and massacres it via a brutal industrial process, the Venkys have transformed the club from debt-free Premier League staples into debt-laden Championship strugglers.

As is almost common to every dodgy owner, Venky's operate a revolving door managerial appointment policy, one that has seen eight managers come and go since they arrived.

Crowd numbers at Ewood Park continue to decline as loyal fans despair at the sight of their best players being sold to cover debts. Meanwhile, an eerie silence has settled over the Rovers boardroom.

4
Alexandre Gaydamak, Ali al-Faraj, Balram Chainrai and Vladimir Antonov
Portsmouth 2006–2013

A cautionary tale for those considering financial overreach and a stark illustration of the EFL's inability to give a s**t who takes over its member clubs. In the blink of an eye Portsmouth went from FA Cup winners and a top-half finish in the Premier League to League Two and the prospect of liquidation.

As they hurtled down the divisions, Portsmouth fans were forced to suffer a succession of dodgy owners and a sorry tale of debt, administration and incompetence.

They even suffered the ignominy, unique in English football if true, of enduring what might be the first example of a fictitious owner.

To this day, there's debate whether al-Faraj ever actually existed. He never met any of the club's directors or EFL officials. In fact, an investigation by the *Spectator Business* magazine failed to find anyone who had ever met him at all.

3
Ken Anderson
Bolton Wanderers 2016–2019

Anderson arrived at Bolton in 2016 as part of a consortium led by former Wanderers forward, Dean Holdsworth.

Within a year, Anderson, who had been disqualified from being a company director between 2005 and 2013, had taken full control. Devoid of resources or anything resembling a plan, debts inevitably rose at the loss-making club. Players and staff regularly went unpaid, as the owner tested the patience of the EFL.

Eventually, after several close calls, administration arrived in 2019. At one point it looked as if the troubled club was on the verge of liquidation and expulsion from the Football League. Luckily, at the last moment, a buyer for the debt-laden Trotters was found, bringing an end to Anderson's three-year reign of malaise.

2
George Reynolds
Darlington 1999–2005

Reynolds bought Darlington in 1999, with the plan to turn the fourth-tier minnows into a Premier League club. He built a multi-million-pound, 25,000-seater stadium, an untenable white elephant that remained outlandishly excessive for Darlington's regular gate of 2,000.

In 2004, Reynolds was arrested and eventually jailed for money laundering. The club was relegated to the National League and went into administration, burdened by the costs incurred by the stadium (which had been partly financed with high-interest loans). Unable to agree a Creditors' Voluntary Agreement, it was ultimately expelled from the FA in 2012.

A new incarnation of the club, initially refused the 'Darlington' name by the FA, was forced to start life in

Division One of the Northern League, the ninth tier of English football.

1
Steve Dale
Bury 2018–2019

Steve Dale achieved the improbable. The destruction of a League One club. Devoid of resources, a plan or anything resembling competence, he bought Bury, a club already on life support, for £1 back in 2018.

The club inevitably hurtled towards disaster. The finances got so bad that games were suspended and, in the absence of anyone willing to come in and take the club off his hands, Bury were eventually expelled from the Football League in 2019.

On expulsion, the club's employees had their contracts invalidated. It left Bury without players, without its coaching staff and without a league to compete in.

Not bad for eight months' work.

V

AR

For years, through gritted teeth, football just about lived with the inconsistencies of refereeing. There was a grudging acceptance that despite the brief spasm of fury that mistakes created, and the lingering resentment some could cause, by and large, with the notable exception of perennial beneficiaries Manchester United and Liverpool, decisions probably evened themselves out over the course of a season.

But in recent decades this consensus has been shredded, undone by petulant managers whinging about every perceived injustice, by over-analytical pundits poring over mistakes to the point of destruction and by fan-fuelled social media whipping up a storm of perspective-free fury.

With the kind of surveillance tools available that the CIA might regard as a little over-intrusive, the footballing powers that be finally responded, delivering unto us the glory that is VAR. Finally, its creators stated, the inconsistencies of refereeing would be removed from the game. VAR would render debate superfluous, so definitive would its judgements be. Its arsenal of camera angles and expert analysis represented a quantum leap on the existing system, one that had been fatally susceptible to human fallibility.

With VAR, not only could it be definitively judged whether a wayward foot or hand was offside, but it would now be possible to see whether a player's arm hair or toenail had gained a telling yet illegal advantage. Your body might be on, VAR could reveal, but what if you had coughed at the vital moment and sent microparticles of spittle into an offside position? This was decision-making at an atomic level.

Of course, it hasn't proven to be so clear-cut. Since its introduction, VAR has often merely added a further level of frustration and inconsistency to the game. Despite apparently helping to improve the accuracy of refereeing decisions across the top flight to 94 per cent (although, unhelpfully, the Premier League won't release the pre-VAR figure), it has frequently given decisions that remain mystifying to players and fans alike.

This, combined with the stop-start nature of VAR and the lack of information provided to those watching and playing, has added to its unpopularity.

Aware of this, and the system's current limitations, rumours emerging from the FA and the Premier League suggest that a new system is already under construction. Taking inspiration from the 2002 Tom Cruise vehicle,

Minority Report, they've set about creating their own 'Precog' unit, a revolutionary approach to the game designed to predict offences before they've even happened. Facts are sketchy, but leaked images of Mike Dean and Jonathan Moss immersed together in a pool of translucent goo suggest that the plans are already well advanced.

Very Pleased to Meet You

The battle is over, everyone has done their best, the contest is left on the pitch. It might, objectively, be a weird gesture – the brief grasping of another human's hand – but the sentiment is sound. It says well done or hard luck, a sign of mutual respect (even if not always sincere).

But before a game? What's the point of that?

Nothing has happened. The players have just come out of the tunnel and jogged on to the pitch. So, in that instance, the handshake's other meaning, one of introduction, beloved of regional sales directors and privately educated men, is the only thing left on the table. Which means the entire handshake routine just acts like one massive introductory exercise, but one in which a load of people who have just spent a minute together in the tunnel, get a chance to say hello, only on a more formal footing.

In defence of the pre-match handshake, Sky and the Premier League often refer to it as a 'tradition'. But can it really be that much of a 'tradition' if it only dates back to 2004? It's like referring to the storied history of MK Dons or the long-held custom of fans waving giant foam fingers at games.

Another part of the defence centres around the issue of respect, and the Premier League's assertion that this is the reason handshaking was introduced in the first place. But that claim is made slightly ridiculous by what happens not long after the handshake takes place, 90 minutes of kicking the s**t out of each other and trying to get opponents sent off.

You suspect that, as is so commonly the case with the Premier League, the introduction of handshaking was really about the 'optics'.

It forms the centrepiece of the pre-match pantomime, a weird moment of choreography that starts with the strange reverence of the ball, which sits there on a podium, like some kind of spherical idol, surveying all before it. Then, as the players and officials run out, this leather god is grasped by the referee, who you half expect to leave in its place a bang of sand, Indiana Jones style.

The ref will transport the idol to the Premier League altar, another weird addition to the pre-match routine, a pop-up place of worship hastily constructed by a legion of scurrying minions. And it's there that the players gather to eventually be introduced to each other.

You can often tell how pointless some aspect of modern football really is if you subtract it and then see whether it makes any difference to the game. And with the pre-match pantomime, the answer is that it makes absolutely no difference at all.

English football managed to do without the handshake for over 100 years. It could probably get along just fine without it for 100 more.

The E**V**il Summer

The evil summer, with its buxom men, its self-satisfied dickheads playing bongos down the park, its permanent stench of sun cream and cremated meat. The hateful summer with its frisbees, its children's laughter, its relentless heat. Death to the summer and its salads, its sunburn and its psychotic wasps.

But more than anything, when it comes to the Premier League, damn the summer for its cultivation of hope. In football, the summer is the promised land, a time when the dross of the recent season finally comes to an end. It's a period of infectious optimism when all of football's happy outcomes remain deliriously possible.

Even the most hardened of footballing pessimists, the kind who will write a season off when the club's star summer signing gives the ball away two minutes into the opening game of the campaign, can't fail to succumb to the sunny optimism of the summer.

These months have a near miraculous quality. You approach the season's end weary, tired of football and all its predictability.

The campaign has chipped away at your reserves of hope. You're ready for a breather.

But the summer does something to you. Not long after the campaign's conclusion, you're resurrected. Like Lazarus rolling back the stone, you emerge anew. And this reborn self is barely recognisable from the world-weary wreck of just a few days ago. Sunshine and optimism are everywhere as you approach the season to come.

This year will be different. This is the season when it all comes good.

But will it? Will it really be the season when it all comes good?

Or, instead, will the summer merely be a prelude to more of the same? A season to pretty much mirror those that have come before.

At the highest levels, English football has never been more predictable than it is now. Between 1960 and 1980, 12 different clubs won the league. In the past 20 years that number has halved. The same lack of variance has hit the FA Cup, with just seven clubs winning it over the past two decades, compared with 14 between 1960 and 1980. And beyond silverware, the higher reaches of the table have become increasingly staid, with only four clubs from outside the 'Big Six' fleetingly crashing the top four since 2000.

Which makes you realise how evil the summer really is, filling us with hope that, for those following clubs beyond the elite, will soon dissipate to nothing.

Is it the worst thing about the summer? No. Because that will always be men's open-toed sandals. But football's seasonal cultivation of false hope comes a close second.

We Want Our Game Back

'Football Without Fans is Nothing', 'Enough is Enough', 'Against Modern Football'. You've all seen the banners. Their message is clear. We've had enough. We want our game back.

We want the clock resetting, the return of the terraces, of cheap tickets, of football going back to its working-class roots.

It's a message that's universally applauded today. As it was five years ago. And five years before that. In fact, for nearly 30 years, millions of us fans have supported it.

But those demands, and that groundswell of support, might carry more power if the banners were unfurled in near-empty stadiums, broadcast to dwindling numbers at home. And yet, year after year, season after season, the stadiums remain jam-packed, the viewing figures bountiful.

Like turkeys voting (and paying) for Christmas, we fans support a system that from our perspective is systematically designed to ruin the game we love and that financially exploits us at every turn.

Imagine paying ever increasing amounts to watch a film that, while rolling, managed to destroy the very idea of cinema, like *Cats* for example. And then moaning about what's happening, while going back to watch *Cats* again and again. 'Film Without Fans is Nothing', your banner will read, as you sit in your expensive cinema seat to watch *Cats* for the 20th time that year.

The reality is that supporter power exists on something of a gradient in English football. At the bottom, in the divisions of the non-league world, fans can have a massive impact on how clubs are run, to the point where supporter ownership has flourished at clubs like Lewes, Tonbridge Angels and FC United of Manchester.

But that sense of influence tends to trickle away as you climb the pyramid. As the sums involved in takeovers grow larger and the size of the apathetic fanbase swells, diluting the impact that supporter activists can have, fan power dissipates. By the time you reach the pinnacle, the glitz and glamour of the Premier League, it has almost disappeared completely.

Not that those of us who cling to the idea of supporter power at the top seem to realise this. The battle for the soul of English football was lost a generation ago, the game sacrificed on the altar of turbo-capitalism. But, like the last Marxists in the Labour Party, organising a Thursday night Q&A with members of the Sandinista Liberation Front, complete with performance poetry from the Wandsworth People's Theatre, we plough on regardless.

Somehow, we've failed to realise that this is the story where the Empire won and all the Ewoks got interned in labour camps, where Biff Tannon just beat the s**t out of Marty McFly, where the velociraptors ate the kids. And for all the retweets and likes on social media, nothing is going to change that.

Wembley

The old Wembley was a bit s**t. It was hard to get to, on its last legs and filled with all the problems that curse many 'traditional' stadiums: inaccessibility, a pervading feeling of discomfort, the worrying sense that bits of it might fall on your head.

But, to mitigate all of that, it still had a feeling of magic, the history that had soaked itself into the brickwork. You could put up with everything that was wrong with Wembley, just to experience the shiver of excitement that walking towards the twin towers gave you.

And then the FA decided to knock it down and build a stadium fit for the 21st century. In doing so they managed to turn something that was a bit s**t into something very s**t.

For a start, despite the inconvenience of Wembley's location, stuck on the outskirts of the capital, accessible only after a long and expensive journey for most fans, the FA decided to build the new 'national' stadium in exactly the same place. No attempt was made to think about being more inclusive, to consider the distance some supporters have to travel. Instead, the FA, in keeping with its general outlook on life, thought that if it was good enough in 1923, it is good enough today.

When drawing up the new designs they then decided to do away with the twin towers, one of the most iconic footballing structures in the English game, if not the world. In their place came the 'Wembley Arch', a part of the structure that nobody has cared about since it was constructed; likely not even the person who designed it.

The new stadium, when it was eventually completed, late and over budget, was everything you would expect a modern ground to be, a brutalist concrete lump devoid of charm. Surrounded by a windswept, concrete plaza that seems to have taken the post-war Soviet Union as its inspiration, it spoke of a design that was all about how it looked on paper and nothing about how it worked in real life.

In keeping with the Soviet aesthetic, on matchdays the plaza is delineated into fan zones, FA-sponsored areas of controlled fun. Mixing isn't permitted. Nor is excessive enjoyment. This is a fan-lite experience, a sanitised version of what it means to be a supporter. You'll have fun, the zones promise, only our definition of fun, and not too much of it.

Once inside, the 'Wembley Experience' doesn't get much better as a labyrinth system of escalators directs people to their seats, like a conveyor belt of the damned. Along the way, you *can* stop off, but only to buy some food and drink from an array of outlets that seem to have taken hotel minibars as their inspiration for pricing.

And then, once in your seat, you get to experience the final ingredient, the 'legendary' Wembley atmosphere. For a ground that holds so many people, Wembley does a great job of sucking the life out of the air. Perhaps they got the acoustics wrong? Maybe the cost of the 'Wembley experience' has excluded those who tend to make the most noise? Or maybe, just maybe, giving too much of the ground over to the corporate crowd has watered down any atmosphere the remainder could conjure up.

When they redeveloped Wembley, the FA wanted it to stand as a physical representation of modern football in England. And, to their credit that's exactly what they delivered: soulless, expensive and irrevocably bland. It's the national stadium that today's game probably deserves.

A Cold, Wet Tuesday Night in Stoke

It's the great leveller, the benchmark against which all (foreign-born) players must be judged, still routinely trotted out to question the character of those from beyond our shores. One thing to do it in August, they say, when the sun is shining, the pitch is perfect and the temperature balmy. But altogether another thing to do it on a cold, wet Tuesday night in Stoke, when the mercury is plummeting and Ryan Shawcross's boot is wedged up your arse.

In fairness, a freezing, wet midweek night in Stoke is a challenging thing. Although, that could be said of any night in Stoke.

But in football terms, 'Stoke' is essentially a proxy, for which any 'grim' northern town could be inserted. The kind of place, so those who value the testing qualities of such a setting contend, that a mercurial, South American winger would find a challenge.

There's undeniably an undercurrent at play here. Seeing this context reveal something undeniably 'British', an unyielding toughness that has long been defined as a quintessential element of English football. For these pundits and writers, the nation's greatest footballing achievement will always be 6 September 1989, Sweden v England and the sight of Terry Butcher continuing to the end, his face bloodied and bandaged. This was the living embodiment of both the 'Bulldog Spirit' and a wanton disregard for basic wound hygiene, apparently the two cornerstones of our nation's footballing character.

The weird thing about the 'Stoke' test is that it suggests that those who come here from abroad have lived a gilded existence, free from struggle. As though the only hardship they had ever encountered was getting their gold boots to fit properly. It assumes that those gentle 'Latin' wingers haven't grown up in grinding poverty, in places so run down and devoid of hope that they make Stoke look like Las Vegas.

And it's only foreign players. Because this measure of tenacity, the ability to get on with it regardless of the conditions, is rarely applied to English players of a similar ilk. They get a free pass, despite plenty of them, season after season, going missing when the going gets Stoke.

Considering its longevity, it's a surprise that this metric, which has been part of the football world for so long, hasn't crossed over into other parts of English cultural life. Yes, he can belt out a libretto at Glyndebourne on a summer's evening Alan, but can he do it during an icy downpour at the Bet365? Sure Brian, we can all admire his mastery of iambic pentameter, but would he manage it with Kevin Wimmer marking him on a wet, November night in the Potteries?

Wimbledon FC's Misadventures in Modern Football

As origin stories go, it's not the best. No radioactive spiders, no misadventures with gamma rays, nobody having adamantium fused to their skeletons. Instead, just naked opportunism and appalling football governance.

Back in 2000, the Milton Keynes Stadium Consortium (MKSC), a group led by the developer, and part-time Mick Hucknall impersonator, Pete Winkelman, put together a proposal for a large commercial and retail development in the town.

The development would include a 30,000-capacity football stadium. Strangely for a town widely regarded as the beating heart of English football, Milton Keynes lacked a local club that could possibly fill anything more than a hundredth of the new ground. And so, Hucknall got creative.

He began looking for struggling clubs that could be lured away from their spiritual homes, tempted by the chance to play in a brand-new stadium and to enjoy the bountiful pleasures of Milton's Keynes's innovative grid road system.

He eventually found the answer to this problem 62 miles away in south London. At the time, Wimbledon were in trouble. Massively in debt, no ground to call their own and with the club's Norwegian owners looking to offload, the offer from Winkelman to buy the Wombles and relocate them to Milton Keynes came at an opportune moment.

The owners quickly accepted. And, for the first time in the English professional game, franchise football became a possibility.

The fans inevitably protested, taking their case to the Football League, believing that sanity would prevail. As if to illustrate from the very beginning that this wouldn't be the case, the League brought in the FA.

The pair put together a panel to consider the matter. It sat for four days, taking contributions from both sides, eventually being won over by Winkelman's 'infectious enthusiasm'. When the final judgement came, it left the supporters crushed. The move would be allowed, meaning Wimbledon would be severing their 113-year association with south London.

In September 2003, the club moved wholesale to Milton Keynes, later being rebranded as MK Dons.

The fans that were left behind did manage to give the story a happy ending of sorts. They founded their own supporter-owned club in the nether regions of non-league football, AFC Wimbledon, which powered up the pyramid and eventually ended up in the same division as their evil twin.

But that twin still remained, a carbuncle on the face of the English game. One of the worst aspects of the MK

Dons story is the fact that over time their presence has been normalised. Franchise football now has a functioning and accepted precedent. And considering the parlous financial state that many football clubs currently find themselves in, you wouldn't bet against it all happening again one day soon.

The Club World Cup

The idea of the Club World Cup is simple: take the winners of the six continental champions leagues, along with the host nation's national champions, and pit them against each other. Like any sane reader of that sentence, before its completion you've probably come up with numerous reasons why this is a terrible idea. But then try telling FIFA that.

In football terms, the whole thing is comically ill-matched. To give you a taste, back in 2018, Oceanic champions, Team Wellington, made it to the competition alongside the likes of Real Madrid and River Plate. Not only are the New Zealanders a semi-pro team, but they're also not even the biggest club in Wellington.

Inevitably, year after year, the minnows never come out on top and the title of 'World Champions' is consistently claimed by the Europeans or the South Americans, who waltz in for the closing stages, the organisers keen to avoid any genuine upsets.

Considering the 'opposition', that mantle of 'World Champions' does seem a little lightweight. It's a bit like claiming to be the country's most empathetic Tory MP or the best-dressed man in Clacton.

But complaining about that or the pointlessness of the competition does sort of miss the point. Because the Club World Cup isn't really about football. It's about FIFA. The whole tournament is exactly the kind of jamboree that football's governing body loves to flog to countries that reside on the game's fringes – countries like recent hosts, Qatar.

It's another opportunity for FIFA to rake in sponsorship revenue, award themselves generous services contracts and – probably – get a few backhanders along the way. The football is by the by.

Which is why the 2019 Club World Cup in Qatar made so much sense. For the Arab state, a country with little football infrastructure, but a palpable desire to use the sport to wash its appalling international reputation, the competition was the perfect vehicle to purchase. And for FIFA, who better to sell it to than a country drowning in money, while at the same time possessing a flexible approach to financial accountability.

Keen to wring ever more amounts of cash from the format, the whole movable feast is set to expand in the coming years. Although the David and Goliath nature of the competition will continue, FIFA is bringing more clubs into the fold, notably from the wealthy European elite. With football's governing body rumoured to be selling the broadcast rights for billions, it seems as though one of the most ridiculous competitions in world football isn't just here to stay, but about to become a much bigger deal.

X Factor

You expect it on *The X Factor*, as some blandly attractive, proto-teen sensation raises their head to stare moodily into the middle distance. You don't expect it from Rob Holding. It just makes it look as if he's woken up from a nap, or that we've caught him out as he was staring down at his feet (likely wondering just what he's supposed to use them for).

The 'heads-up' has become such an entrenched part of football broadcasting that it's hard to believe that there was a time when it never existed. But there was. In the distant past, players were just interviewed or profiled. At no point did the interview or montage piece require a slow motion, two-second clip of the player in question first looking down and then bringing his head up to look directly into the camera.

But, led by Sky, the practice has now become ubiquitous in the modern game.

In general, broadcasters might just about get away with it if the player in question is some deliriously captivating, attacking magician, like Ronaldo or Messi. Or even when it's a deliciously tempting specimen of manhood, the kind that might make even the most robustly confirmed of heterosexual males reconsider their life choices, such as Graziano Pelle or Andre Gomes. But when it's Phil Jones, it just feels jarring.

That same sense of dissonance is also on show in another of Sky's recent visual innovations, the expanded team line-up. Apparently, somebody at Sky towers thought that just putting out a team sheet was no longer good enough. Instead, we now have the various players in a team's sections of the pitch – defence, midfield, attack – revealed to us like the members of a boy band, each striking a pre-rehearsed pose. There's the funny one, there's the handsome one, there's Harry Maguire.

Somebody at Sky has clearly been watching far too much *X Factor*. So much so that you wonder where it will all end? Olly Murs as anchor? Every player profile to include a tear-inducing back story set to 'Hello' by Adele? It promises to be a bleak future if we continue on this path.

E**X**iting Early

We've all done it and, objectively, leaving the match early can make complete sense. Sacrificing those closing minutes can mean no queuing at the station or the bus stop, getting to the pub handy, arriving home at a reasonable hour.

And sometimes, if your team is getting a pasting in a game of little significance and it's so cold that it's been about 30 minutes since you felt your toes, all of the above is so alluring that you would have to question the sanity and reason of anyone who stays put and sticks it out to the bitter end.

But since when did football have anything to do with sanity or reason? If it did, none of us would ever go to the match in the first place, parting with stupid amounts of money with no guarantee of happiness. Football is unreasonable and ridiculous. Like believing in an afterlife, it's also an act of faith.

And leaving early is the death of faith.

Odds-on, when you scarper five minutes before the end, you're probably not going to miss much. Generally, games aren't turned on their head during injury time. Normally you have a feeling which way a match is going long before the final whistle.

But sometimes surprises do occur. There are the famous examples, such as Agüero's injury-time winner to give Manchester City the title in 2012. And then there are the less epoch-shattering, such as Newcastle United's two injury-time goals to escape with a draw at Goodison Park during the 2019/20 season.

These are the outcomes, however improbable, that we give up on when we nip out a few minutes before the end, moments of delirium that, whether titanic like Agüero's or just immensely satisfying like Newcastle's, will go on to form a vital part of your club's grand narrative.

And anyway, what exactly are you doing with the extra time saved? Unravelling the mysteries of the known universe? Finding a cure for the common cold? Reaching a transcendental state beyond name and form? Or, like me, are you sitting on the sofa in a trackie, staring vacantly at the TV while shovelling biscuits down your neck?

Is all that really worth the death of faith? Obviously, it depends on the biscuits, but probably not.

E**X**tremist Lads

Of all the things to bring back from the 1930s why did it have to be fascism? Why couldn't it be other stuff that was all the rage back then, such as travelling by airship or youth hostelling?

In the last few years, a plethora of far-right parties and movements, such as the English Defence League and Britain First, have emerged in this country. All of these have, to various degrees, tried to swell their ranks with disaffected white nationalists drawn from the remnants of the hooligan network, the kind of people who love white supremacy almost as much as they love Lonsdale.

Of the groups that have emerged and operated like this, none have done it more explicitly than the Football Lads Alliance (FLA).

Founded back in 2017 in response to several terrorist attacks in the UK, but specifically the bombing of Manchester Arena, the FLA claimed that it was avowedly apolitical. But if you're going to make claims like that, it's probably best not to affiliate with known far-fight figures such as Tommy Robinson and attempt to build alliances with other far-right groups such as Generation Identity.

Just to maintain the whole extremist movement vibe, specifically the way that extremists love splintering over contentious points of theory, the FLA has even endured a split. Not long after its founding, a new group, the Democratic Football Lads Alliance, hived off following an argument over the finer points of racism. It's quite hard to differentiate between the two groups but, if I've read it right, one believes in the supremacy of whites and the other in white supremacy.

The sad truth is that football has got form when it comes to the far right. Back in the 1970s and early 1980s it was the National Front forging connections with the hooligan firms of England. The image back then of the Chelsea skinhead, NF tattoo carved into his arm, an array of racial prejudices colouring his worldview, was a stereotype that depressingly had its roots in reality.

As the hooligan firms were clamped down upon during the late 1980s and the 1990s it was hoped that the problem had been eradicated from the game completely. Clearly it was just dormant. Starting with the English Defence League in 2009, the re-emergence of hooligan firms on the game's fringes with far-right sympathies has illustrated that modern football once again has a fascist problem.

Which leads me back to the many alternative delights of the 1930s. Imagine how much better the world would be if rather than investing their time in espousing moronic racist beliefs and peddling hate, these 'Football Lads' got really into blimps instead.

And, if you really had to, in the spirit of compromise, you could even make the blimps white. Come on 'Football Lads', we're meeting you halfway here …

You Only Sing When You're Organised in a Club-Sanctioned Singing Section

Aware that many grounds in the top flight were becoming quieter than a library on matchdays, clubs have been wracking their brains to think up new ways to tackle the problem. Or at least ways that don't include making ticket prices low enough to allow young, vocal scallies back into the ground (the ones who actually do the singing).

Even managers have got in on the act. Sold on the idea that the Premier League had the 'most passionate fans in the game', the likes of Jürgen Klopp and Antonio Conte have been genuinely surprised to rock up at their respective grounds and find nothing but apathy. In response, they've tried to shame supporters into acting and, on occasion, attempted to physically whip them up in a frenzy by frenetically parading around their technical areas, like a pub psychopath, spoiling for a fight at last orders.

All too often it has little effect because the demographics of the standard Premier League crowd, which with each passing year look more and more like the average clientele of a Harvester, mitigate against outward displays of passion.

Undeterred by this reality and the crushing realisation that no amount of handclappers can persuade a 40-year-old male to get excited, several clubs, such as Manchester City and Manchester United, have experimented with singing sections.

The hope is that if they can corral together enough of those remaining few willing to sing, then maybe, collectively, they'll at least ensure that some noise is made, their unified voices replacing the sporadic pockets of sound that characterise most home games.

But there's something undeniably sad about the move, the fact that things have got so bad that crowds now need to be socially engineered to elicit something that once came so naturally.

Although, at least it's not as bad as West Ham's rumoured solution to the problem. Back in 2016, according to an array of Hammers fans, the club deployed the use of 'crowd noise' from the dying days of Upton Park through its tannoy system in a bid to enhance the atmosphere at the London Stadium.

Quite why they had a recording of 35,000 angry cockneys telling Sullivan and Gold to 'f**k off' is a mystery. But the noise that was pumped out had no chance of working anyway. And that's because the London Stadium has no atmosphere to begin with and, as science tells us, sound can never travel through a vacuum.

You Spin Me Right Round

You wouldn't think that people who only train for a few hours a day and whose actual 'job' lasts for about 90 minutes would get that tired. But apparently, despite being in the prime of life, cared for by the best medical staff available and training since childhood to do exactly this job, elite footballers find it a challenge to play twice a week. Rotation has become the norm in the higher reaches of the game, with some players rarely trusted to play more than two or three games on the bounce.

The modern master of the art is unquestionably Pep Guardiola, a man who seems to possess a near-pathological need to fiddle with his team, rotating almost as a matter of instinct. It's rumoured within football that so meticulous and meddlesome does Guardiola become that most players can only tolerate him for around three seasons. Eventually, the intensity, the obsessiveness and the luxurious knitwear just become too much.

There are occasions when teams really go for it, usually in the early rounds of the two domestic cups, when top-flight clubs field sides staffed by the first XI's unwanted and those barely old enough to shave. And all to give their brightest and best a breather.

It never used to be like this, so the misty-eyed romantics tell us. In the old days, men were men. Men with simple, honest names such as Dave or John, who would play 2,000 games in a season, wearing boots that weighed more than concrete and on pitches that were basically quagmires. They were the kind of men who would recoil at the idea of wearing skins and who would question the sexuality of anyone choosing to don a pair of gloves. Powered by a diet of unfiltered cigarettes, brown ale and lard, these stalwarts of the game would play every match they could.

But those men are no more, gone to run firmly heterosexual pubs in the sky. In their place have come their pampered descendants, a mollycoddled generation of footballers, who, like a Victorian lady swooning in response to a breach of social etiquette, wither at the prospect of playing a midweek League Cup tie against Lincoln City at Sincil Bank.

Perhaps accommodating the fragile nature of this new kind of player finally gives us the answer to the question that has haunted the game for so long: why don't modern footballers look as old as those from the past?

Flick through Panini sticker books from the 1970s and 1980s and it's like you're scanning through an analogue version of Grindr for the elderly. With their ravaged faces, greying hair and receding hairlines, most footballers looked like Wilfrid Brambell before they had turned 30. Whereas today's bunch seem to age far better, possibly because they're no longer forced to play so many fixtures.

Although, that doesn't account for Charlie Adam.

You'll Never Believe ...

For a start, it's not our fault. Our brains are hard-wired to love clickbait.

It's all down to the 'information-gap' theory. Apparently, whenever we perceive a 'gap' between what we know and what we don't know, it has emotional consequences, creating 'deprivation curiosity'. The curious individual is motivated to obtain the missing information to reduce or eliminate the feeling of deprivation because not knowing is cognitively uncomfortable.

And that means, although at no point in your life have you wondered which dogs modern footballers look most like, when presented with the possibility of finding out, almost without knowing why, you find yourself clicking away.

That's how they get you, preying on your need for information to draw you into a world of adverts, pop-ups and videos that cause your browser to freeze. These aren't articles designed to expand your understanding of football. They're simply a way to exploit that need to know in the hope of driving you to the site's advertisers.

But as awful as they are, sadly, they remain enticing. After all, who amongst us could resist clicking on to the following ...

10 Footballers Who Look Like Their Pets! 15 Players Who Are Known for Something Outside Football! 25 Footballers Who Retired Too Soon! The 12 Premier League Players Most Likely to Spontaneously Combust! 11 Footballers Who Turned to Cannibalism! 7 Goalkeepers Who Have Vestigial Tails! The 35 Footballers Currently Being Investigated for War Crimes! 5 Defenders Who Never Really Existed! The 3 Premier League Stars Who Consumed Their Twin In-utero, 19 Former Players Who

Now Reproduce Asexually! The 22 Footballers Who Know Where You Live! The 9 Ex-Players Who Cultivate Their Own Yeast!

Zealotry

What would it take for us modern fans to see fault with our clubs? The murder of a close relative? The kidnap of a child? An admission that they liked jazz?

Somewhere along the way, we've decided to make irrationality a key part of what it means to be loyal. To question is to go against the faith. There's no room for heretics within the modern game.

You could imagine that the good people behind Scientology must look on in wonder, trying to work out how they too could instil such a ridged sense of adherence amongst their followers. It's almost as though a cult-like aesthetic has descended upon the game, so much so that we can't be that far away from someone like David Gold setting up their own 'Jim Jones' style community, maybe out in Canvey Island, a place where the love is free, the pie and mash plentiful and Mark Noble is venerated as a demigod.

To get slightly psychoanalytic, it all comes down to ego. We have such a brittle sense of self-esteem that admitting our clubs could be in the wrong is intolerable for our egos. And because of that, our mind's defence mechanism kicks into action, distorting perception to make reality less threatening, protecting our fragile egos by changing the very facts in our mind.

The mental gymnastics involved are, at times, something to behold. Liverpool supporters showing solidarity with Luis Suarez after he was found guilty of making racist comments. Spurs fans ringing in to defend their club's decision to furlough non-playing staff.

Impressively, we're not just able to distort reality to protect our fragile egos, we can also hold conflicting points of view. So, Chelsea supporters can, on the one hand, defend their captain John Terry after he was found guilty of making racist comments, while on the other, praise their club a few years later for taking an active role in the Premier League's recent support for the Black Lives Matter campaign.

It's a bit like discovering that Tommy Robinson was secretly a Salafist Imam or turning on the TV to find out that Nigel Farage is the latest member of Diversity.

But should it be like this? Should support really require unquestioning loyalty? These are football clubs after all, not the Moonies. Surely, it's okay to think that Luis Suarez is a racist dickhead or that furloughing staff, while at the same time spending millions in the transfer market, is not okay. Maybe it's time we were fans not fanatics, capable of calling out our clubs when they, inevitably, make mistakes?

Year **Z**ero

At first glance, there's not much to link the Leninist revolutionary and instigator of the Cambodian genocide, Pol Pot, with the former chief executive of the Premier League and one-time Terry from Brookside lookalike, Rick Parry. But each, at one vital point in their lives, embraced a 'clear-the-decks' approach to history.

For the former, this meant a physical return to the land. Urban living was forcibly abandoned in Cambodia, as the country started from scratch, the implementation of 'Year Zero'. It was all part of Pot's deranged vision of building a new, socialist utopia from the bottom up.

For the latter, who acted as midwife to the creation of England's elite division, the arrival of the Premier League represented a clean break from everything that had gone before, English football's very own 'Year Zero'. Over 100 years of footballing history was to be erased in the blink of an eye.

While the brutal repression of Pot's Khmer Rouge would ultimately end in failure, Parry's and the Premier League's lighter touch repression has been an unparalleled success. England's elite division has spent the past few decades, in conjunction with the fiercely loyal Sky and BT, routinely hammering home the same message: football did not exist before 1992.

In an Orwellian rewriting of history, the propaganda machine of the Premier League has steamrollered everything before it. All records now date from 1992. Think that Dixie Dean holds the record for most goals scored in a top-flight season? Well you're wrong, that title belongs to

Alan Shearer and Andy Cole. Think Liverpool have won the league 19 times? Think again, it's just the once.

When, back in 2016, the fans of Leicester City taunted supporters from the likes of Everton, Sunderland and Aston Villa about their lack of league titles, the full scale of the Premier League's 'doublethink' was laid bare. The fact that between them those taunted clubs had won the league 22 times meant nothing under the new reality.

But what to do about it? Pol Pot's grisly adventures in oppression were only brought to an end when neighbouring Vietnam invaded the country. Could a neighbouring force be on hand to do the same to the Premier League? The Cymru Premier? The Scottish Premier? The SSE Airtricity League? It seems unlikely.

So, resistance must come from within. Listen to that quiet voice at the back of your mind that tells you that it is Jimmy Greaves who has scored the most top-flight goals in English football, not Alan Shearer. That it is Peter Shilton who boasts the most senior appearances in the top division, not Gareth Barry.

With their swirling graphics, their bright lights and their remorseless 'on-message' pundits, the Premier League and their media minions will have you doubting yourself, gaslighting faith in your own sanity. But you must be strong. Resistance is not futile.

Zillionaires

Considering that the Premier League rakes in billions in TV income each year and the fact that football clubs, certainly in the higher reaches of the game, are multi-million-pound businesses, it doesn't seem that unfair to think that the people who actually put the graft in should see a decent cut of what's made.

Football is that rarest of things, an industry in which working-class lads can rise to the top and get a decent share of the wealth being created. It's a weirdly redistributive element for an industry that's essentially market capitalism on steroids, the kind of hands-off free-for-all that Milton Friedman would have had wet dreams about.

But for some, this just isn't on. The amounts that footballers earn is regularly criticised by politicians and people in the media, held up as an example of an industry out of control.

The latest to do this was Conservative politician, and John Christie tribute act, Matt Hancock, who, during the first coronavirus lockdown, singled out footballers, suggesting they put their hands in their pockets for the NHS. Not bankers, not hedge fund managers, not property developers – just footballers.

There's often a hint of snobbery about this, a pernicious top-down sense of discrimination that's more about who is earning the money, not what they earn. Because those same voices don't seem to have a problem when other parts of British society, notably the alumni of the country's fee-paying schools, rake in millions each year.

Admittedly, footballers don't do themselves any favours, indulging in some of the worst examples of conspicuous consumerism you'll ever witness. When you see them pictured proudly in front of incalculably expensive sports cars, roaming around their cavernous, gold-leafed mansions, or watching their 200-foot televisions, that sense of working-class solidarity does take something of a hit.

But the fact is, rich people have always bought stuff and the stuff they buy is often disgustingly opulent. Is the above any different to one of the landed aristocracy being pictured in front of their 800-bedroomed country pile? A dead-eyed city trader blowing more than you earn in a year on a diamond-encrusted designer watch? Or members of the elite shelling out a small fortune to take part in a human hunt?

By the time footballers reach an age where they're raking in millions, and it's a small minority that do, they've put in years of hard work and sacrifice, likely much more than the bloated progeny of the country's mansioned class.

You, like me, might not agree that football should be generating so much cash in the first instance, or that so much of the money that's made is in the hands of a tiny minority, but of all the millionaires that this disgustingly lopsided country creates, those few working-class lads that have made it to the top are probably the least deserving of criticism.

Zlatan

'I don't want to be a lion; I am a lion.'

True. Like other lions, Zlatan Ibrahimović is typically found wandering the vast African savannahs. He also mostly socialises by licking and eats 18lbs of meat a day.

With the exception of the licking thing, of course this isn't true. It's just Zlatan being Zlatan. Essentially, what happens when a messiah complex becomes good at football.

Imagine a Venn diagram, with one circle illustrating self-aggrandising bulls**t and the other raging egomania. Where those two circles intersect, that's where you find Zlatan (likely asserting how much better the intersection is by virtue of having him present in it).

The Swede has been a part of the football firmament for two decades now, most of it spent at the top of the game. The Netherlands, Italy, Spain, France, England – Zlatan has played and picked up trophies across the Continent, collecting a haul of silverware that most footballers could only dream of.

But it's not enough for Zlatan to just let his success speak for itself. No, he has to continually speak for his success, wherever and whenever possible. Like one endless and repetitive boast, Ibrahimović never seems happier than when he's telling the world just how magnificent he is.

And frequently in the third person. Illeism or 'being an irritating t**t', as third-person speaking is more commonly known, is without doubt one of the most annoying habits any person can acquire. It might even be worse than telling people your dreams in long and excruciating detail.

In truth, Ibrahimović is exceptionally fortunate that he's an accomplished footballer. Obviously not as good as he thinks he is, because no human ever could be, but very good, nonetheless. Imagine possessing all that ego, believing that you were a divine entity and then only being as good as Clayton Donaldson.

But it's going to stop. There's going to be a time in the not-too-distant future when his ability will fade. You have to fear for Zlatan when that happens. Because, after all, he's a lion, and usually when lions get old and knackered, the pride kick them out. Those poor ragged souls are then left to wander the wilderness alone, with no one to lick for company. What's Zlatan and his god-complex going to do then?

Pundit Zoo

For its aesthetic purity nothing could beat watching the scores via Teletext on a Saturday afternoon. The screen stared back at you, an emotion- and spectacle-free void. You would sit in silence, tension building as the time without change stretched on. And then a near-imperceptible flicker. Your heart rate jumped in response. Something had happened. Your eyes scanned the page in search of the alteration. Found it! Everton had conceded.

If Teletext lies at one extreme of the broadcasting spectrum, surely its ultimate replacement, Pundit Zoo, lies at the other. On Sky and BT, the format is the same. Put a handful of pundits in a room, dial back the conventional studio formality by about 40 per cent, chuck in a ringleader to vaguely orchestrate proceedings and then let the fun times roll.

Ostensibly, the pundits are there to describe the action that you can't see, acting as your emotional proxy. They wince at every miss, cheer with every goal. If you had ever wondered how you might react to your team scoring if you were able to experience football through an act of soul bonding with Paul Merson, a question all of us have pondered from time to time, then wonder no more.

But that's only part of why the zoo has been assembled. Just as important is the 'atmosphere'. Sky and BT know that the modern football world they've helped create has effectively priced many out of going to the match. But have no fear. Through their innovative creation of 'Bantervision', they can bring the experience of being at the game to the comfort of your own home.

The in-jokes, the nicknames, the sense of false bonhomie, it's just like the real thing (if you had somehow ended up at the match with someone you didn't like). It's all about having a laugh, not taking things too seriously. It's the 'fun-time' uncle of sports broadcasting, the kind of uncle who arrives at your birthday party pissed, vomits over the cat and ends up passed out on your sister's bed.

Despite its apparent half-arsed appearance, the truth is that a lot of work goes into 'Bantervision'. The reduced formality it replaces is put together painstakingly, ingredient by ingredient – a pinch of locker room, a dash of suburban golf club, a hint of pending sexual harassment lawsuit – the whole mix coalescing to create a kind of pre-watershed men's club, a destination every bit as depressing as that sounds.

Epilogue

AFTER ALL that moaning, it's probably only fair to end with a list of some of the good things about modern football, because despite all the inequality, the financial madness, the Paul Pogba clothing ranges, it's not all bad. Stuff like …

Richarlison always looking pissed off. Marcelo Bielsa's bucket. Bournemouth finally getting relegated. 'Athletico Mince'. Erling Haaland interviews. Leighton Baines. View from the Allotment End. Lewes FC. Marcus Rashford. Night games under the lights. *These Football Times*. AFC Wimbledon. Dulwich Hamlet. Pat Nevin. 'Quickly Kevin, Will He Score?' FC United of Manchester. Curry and chips before the game. Inverting the Pyramid. Barry Glendenning. Messi in flight. *Mundial*. The early rounds of the FA Cup. Alex Scott. AFC Unity. The big moths at the 2018 Euros Final. Ben Godfrey. Aston Villa 7 Liverpool 2. Sunday League. Mark Chapman. Taking your son to the match. TIFO Football. James Richardson. Clapton Ultras. A bullet header from the perfect cross. Trade Union Football & Alcohol Committee. The Dripping Pan. *When Saturday Comes*. Michael Calvin. 1980s Bundesliga kits. Goodison's nuclear hot tea. Elis James.

@DirtyFootballer. *Sunderland 'Til I Die*. *The Guardian* 'Football Weekly'. Route one goals. Vivianne Miedema. 'The Swiss Ramble'. Jürgen Klopp at Dortmund (but not Liverpool). Common Goal. *The Blizzard*. *The Football Pink*. James Rodriguez playing for Everton.